Also by

FRANK WATERS

FICTION

Fever Pitch (1930)
The Wild Earth's Nobility (1935)
Below Grass Roots (1937)
The Dust Within the Rock (1940)
People of the Valley (1941)
The Man Who Killed the Deer (1942)
River Lady (1942)
with Houston Branch
The Yogi of Cockroach Court (1947)
Diamond Head (1948)
with Houston Branch
The Woman at Otowi Crossing (1966)
Pike's Peak (1972)
Flight from Fiesta (1986)

NONFICTION

Midas of the Rockies (1937)
The Colorado (1946)
Masked Gods (1950)
The Earp Brothers of Tombstone (1960)
Book of the Hopi (1963)
Robert Gilruth (1963)
Leon Gaspard (1964)
Pumpkin Seed Point (1969)
To Possess the Land (1973)
Mexico Mystique (1975)
Mountain Dialogues (1981)
Eternal Desert (1990)

BRAVE ARE MY PEOPLE

Brave
Are My People

✚

INDIAN HEROES

NOT

FORGOTTEN

✚

Frank Waters

✚

FOREWORD BY

VINE DELORIA, JR.

✚

Clear Light Publishers

SANTA FE

Clear Light Publishers
823 Don Diego
Santa Fe, New Mexico 87501

LIBRARY OF CONGRESS CATALOGING IN PUBLICATION DATA

Waters, Frank, 1902–
    Brave are my people: Indian heroes not forgotten/Frank Waters;
foreword by Vine Deloria, Jr.
        p.   cm.
    Includes bibliographical references.
    ISBN 0–940666–21–9: $24.95
        1. Indians of North America — Biography. 2. Indians of North
America — History. 1. Title
E 89.W37 1992
920'. 009297—do20   92–53961
[B]   CIP

First edition
10 9 8 7 6 5 4 3 2 1

Printed in U.S.A. by Publishers,Press, Salt Lake City, Utah

♻ Printed on recycled paper which meets the minimum requirements of American National Standard for Information Sciences — Permanence of Paper for printed library materials, ANSIZ39, 48–1984.

Contents

List of Plates

Foreword

Biography, if done properly, reduces the distance between the great
acts and actors of history — and between us, the readers, and these
acts and actors — so that we come to see incarnate in a person's life
the temper and sequence of an age. Frank Waters, the premier writer
of the American West, has combined biography and history to sketch
an incarnational history of the past five hundred years. Drawing on
many sources and reconstructing scenes and conversations, Waters
offers portraits of brave Indian leaders who personify the dispossession
of the indigenous peoples of the Western Hemisphere. He does not
glorify these men so much as he reminds us of the pain, isolation,
nobility, and ultimately the futility of fighting against men, machines,
and the passage of time.

Reading these tragic stories, the question arises: Could it have been
different during the past five centuries? Couldn't there have been
some more humane way to bring European civilization and religion
to the remote reaches of our planet? Expressions of regret over the
past can include a multitude of insights for us to reflect upon. However, human beings will probably continue to dispossess and abuse
each other until we reach a cosmic consciousness and take our place
in the larger universe. We will need to reach deep inside ourselves if
we are to achieve this status — and here Frank Waters is an important
thinker, and this book becomes a critical signpost on our road to
species maturity.

We have no sense of nobility, gentility, or integrity today; and
unfortunately, we have no models in the personal lives of our citizens from which to take our cues. These Indian leaders, however —

Tecumseh, Mangas Coloradas, and the rest — had a sense of personal worth, of a mission to be accomplished, and of a relationship with the life forces of the greater cosmos in a measure that we have not seen since. Fighting overwhelming odds, suffering the loneliness of knowing the situation was hopeless, and maintaining their sense of person was an achievement few of us can conceive and none of us can match.

Frank Waters sketches the impossible dream of our existence in this book: How can we maintain a sense of personal dignity and refuse to surrender to the inevitable forces of change that can at any minute engulf us in meaningless catastrophes? Imagine the inner feelings of these Indian leaders who, not fearing death, at the same time lived their lives until the very end, and thereby ensured that their lives counted in the midst of utterly senseless change. We must likewise be true to ourselves, to what we know of ourselves, and to those principles we admire. In that way, we force history to move around us, and do not allow it to move over us.

Frank has saved his best and deepest book for the last part of his writing career, and for this we should thank him. Whatever we have learned from everything else that he has written, we find it coalesced here in these simple portraits of men who looked destiny in the face and changed forever what it had in mind. I personally would like nothing more than to walk into Frank's chapters with a weapon and stand at the side of these noble men as they breathe their last — a second with a real person is better than a long life with people who cannot take a chance and live their dreams and ideals. In the end, of course, the character of Frank Waters that we have all admired for so long is found in these chapters, and his kinship with the men who made the past five centuries of American history is affirmed. Thanks, Frank.

Vine Deloria, Jr.
Boulder, Colorado

Preface

THE TITLE of this book, *Brave Are My People*, is taken from a speech by the great Shawnee warrior-statesman Tecumseh given before the Osages in 1800.

It could well apply to members of all tribes, and to my father, Frank Jonathon Waters, who was part Cheyenne. In my semi-autobiographical novel *Pike's Peak* (1971), I devoted a lengthy section of the narrative to an account of the few years I knew him; he died when I was twelve years old. He was about six feet tall, slimly built, with straight black hair, high cheekbones, and swarthy skin. A simple, caring man.

My boyhood home of Colorado Springs, Colorado, in the first decade of the new century, was a noted scenic resort and health spa, drawing visitors from all over the country. Gold had been discovered along Cripple Creek on the slope of Pike's Peak, and the town was getting rich, the fashionable North End filling with impressive mansions.

The neighborhood where Father, Mother, my younger sister Naomi, and I lived was on the east side. Our rented house on El Paso Street fronted the Santa Fe Railroad embankment. We children loved to watch the trains roar by, but Mother kept placing damp newspapers under the windowsills to keep out the rain of cinders. A block west along Bijou Street and the little stream called Shook's Run stood the large gaunt house of my mother's father, Joseph Dozier, a building contractor.

Colorado Springs was not a working man's town, and Father always had trouble finding jobs to support us. For a spell, pedaling a bicycle around to collect premiums, he sold life insurance. Still wearing his sheath knife, he even stood for a week behind a necktie counter in a haberdashery. Whenever Grandfather had a construction job, Father operated the cement mixer; and after Grandfather opened a mine at Cripple Creek, Father often helped him.

Father's great break came one summer when he was called to the remote trading post of Hon-Not-Klee, "Shallow Water," on the immense Navajo Reservation in New Mexico. Bruce, the trader, was ill and needed help. Father took me with him. It was easy to see how quickly he fitted in with life among the Navajos, learning a smattering of their language and the tricks they tried to play on him. In no time he won their respect and friendship, this "tall, dark man at Shallow Water." But it was no place for Mother, my sister, and me.

Home again, Father resumed the worrying job of hunting work. Every dollar he brought home was a testimonial to his love for his family. He was proud of us, and we were proud of him.

Sundays he spent with his family. We would ride the streetcar to Manitou Springs, at the base of Pike's Peak, and fill our jugs and bottles with soda and iron water from the many springs. An alternate Sunday outing was to take the trolley car line to Stratton Park at the foot of Cheyenne Mountain. Here was a playground where we children could amuse ourselves. Then we would have a picnic lunch up one of the canyons.

On weekends when Father wasn't working, he would spend some time with his best friend, a Cheyenne vegetable huckster named Indian Joe. Father in his neat suit and shined boots loved to ride on the plank seat of Indian Joe's rickety wagon when the old man, huddled in his dirty blanket, made his rounds.

Father often visited the nearby Ute encampment. The Utes had been moved to a reservation in the mountains, but a band of them was permitted every summer to return to their old home. Their smoke-grey lodges were pitched on the mesa west of town. Father would take me with him of an evening. He would squat with the circle of men around the cooking fire. With his long-bladed sheath knife, he, too, would slice a pink slab off the roast and eat it in his fingers, while the women and we children would wait our turn at table.

More and more often he was called up to Cripple Creek to work in our "Family Folly," Grandfather's sylvanite mine. Each time, Father returned looking more tired and wan. He was a man of space, of wide sunlit plains and prairies, not the dark damp depths of a granite stope of a mine eleven thousand feet high on the slope of Pike's Peak.

There came the day he returned home on a cot in the baggage car of the Cripple Creek Short Line. At home he was put to bed in the downstairs living room, where a neighborhood practical nurse helped Mother take care of him. A few nights later he died. A man who had accepted without complaints the obscure and difficult role life had assigned him. A man brave enough to be gentle. His influence upon me I have appreciated more every year.

*   *   *

I want to take this opportunity to thank all those who helped to prepare this book for publication. My wife Barbara Ann Waters deserves special mention. As for all my later books, she served virtually as my memory and right hand throughout the entire course of the work involved. Marcia Keegan and Harmon Houghton, of Clear Light Publishers, took the risk of publishing my old manuscript, ignored for years because I didn't consider it among my better work. Dennis Dutton, an old friend, as editor helped to bring it up to date. Howard Bryan, a friend of many years, Joe Sando of Jemez Pueblo, and Alfonso Ortiz of San Juan Pueblo, all fellow writers, read the manuscript and corrected details when necessary. My thanks also to others too numerous to mention separately.

I can't say how deeply the beautiful foreword by Vine Deloria, Jr., touches me. Since the publication of *Custer Died for Your Sins: An Indian Manifesto* in 1969, Vine has been the leading voice of Indian America. None other is listened to so closely. As a close friend, I have respected and admired him for many years. Now, reading his words upon my own writing, I feel how much he and his opinion mean to me; and I can gratefully acknowledge his foreword only by saying in return, thanks, Vine.

Frank Waters
Taos, New Mexico

Introduction

THIS IS A BOOK of flashing glimpses, each lasting maybe five to ten pages, of a series of American Indians whose lives have enriched the history of America.

They appear geographically from the Atlantic to the Pacific and chronologically from 1600 to 1900, following Anglo America's westward expansion and its conquest of Indian America.

It was Chief Seattle who spoke the epitaph of all the tribes defeated in defense of their homelands. The occasion was his oration before Isaac Stephens, governor of the Territory of Washington, when he gave up his Duwamish tribe's homelands and accepted confinement on a reservation. The year was 1859, almost two decades before the Nez Percé tribe finally surrendered its own homeland in Oregon. Still to come was the ghastly massacre at Wounded Knee, which in 1890 finally ended Indian armed resistance to the flood of incoming Anglos.

Chief Seattle's oration may be the most famous of all Indian orations. It is not only the epitaph of his race, spoken without sadness or bitterness: "Tribe follows tribe, and nation follows nation, like the waves of the sea. It is the order of nature, and regret is useless." It is also prophetic, with a warning to the white victors: "Your time of decay may be distant, but it will surely come; for even the White Man . . . cannot be exempt from the common destiny."

This quiet declamation speaks with the voice of the "Being Within, communing with past ages," as it was called by another great Indian orator, the Shawnee Chief Tecumseh. With its spiritual authority and universality, Seattle's oration should be read in its entirety (pages

181–183), for it assured both Indians and whites that they were entering a change of worlds.

The present 1992 quincentennial of Columbus's first touching the shore of America at San Salvador reminds us of the continent's inhabitants, to whom he mistakenly gave the name of "Indians." Radio and television, the press, and government and business spokesmen are loudly and proudly declaiming the prominent viewpoint that the United States developed from scratch into the richest, most material-istic and powerful nation in world history. All they say is true. But what they don't say about Indians is also true.

No one knows how many Indians were in North America when Columbus arrived. A responsible estimate is one and one-half million. Deven A. Mihesuah, a former Ford Foundation dissertation fellow and a professor of American Indian history, asserts in the *Phi Kappa Phi Journal*, Spring 1991 issue, that there were five million. Continual warfare during Anglo America's march of empire, confinement on reservations, death from diseases brought to America by the white man, poverty, and alcoholism kept reducing them, until by 1910 there were only two hundred and twenty thousand survivors.

Many had believed that the "Vanishing Red Man" would disap-pear entirely by the end of the century, taking his traditions and culture with him. Instead, the Indian population increased to two million in 1990. But they still suffer prejudice, injustice, the lowest poverty level in the country, and substandard health, education, and living conditions. The school dropout rate is three times that of whites. The average age of Indians living on reservations is twenty-one years, and the age of death has been averaging forty-three years.

Enough statistics. The significant meaning is the phenomenal comeback Indians have made against the greatest odds imaginable. Still preserving their love of the land, their sense of unity with all other forms of life, they have become an integral part of the national commonwealth.

So much for the Indians in this "change of worlds." What have the conquering Anglos accomplished as custodians of the vast, new, beautiful land they have gained?

How enchantingly diverse the landscapes of North America once were, with range upon range of snowcapped mountains, lush prairies, illimitable plains of shortgrass, giving way to tawny, sunbaked deserts and fetid jungles, all teeming with life in every form: tiny plants and dense forests, birds, reptiles and insects, and countless species of animals, including the buffalo whose great herds blackened the plains. All of these, too, Indians believed, were children of their common Mother Earth and so had equal rights to life. They supplied the needs of men and women, but they were not sacrificed needlessly and wantonly. And always the Indians ritually obtained their consent to their sacrifice. So, too, was the land regarded as sacred and inviolate, being their Mother Earth. With it and all other forms of life, the Indians knew themselves as a part of one living whole.

The Christian Anglo newcomers held a dramatically different view. Perhaps it came from the first chapter of Genesis in the Judeo-Christian Bible, in which Man was divinely commanded to "subdue" the earth. That was exactly what the white conquerors did as they proceeded westward. They leveled whole forests under the axe, plowed under the grasslands, dammed and drained the rivers, gutted the mountains for gold and silver, and divided and sold the land itself. Accompanying all this destruction was the extermination of birds and beasts, not alone for profit or sport, but to indulge in a wanton lust for killing.

The result of this rapacious onslaught is all too evident now, at least to environmentalists and a mixed bag of worried scientists: the destruction of the land itself, contamination of rivers, lakes, and bounding oceans, pollution of the air to the extent that toxic alarms are frequently sounded in all large cities . . . the entire nation and all its natural resources converted into ready cash! Even Ripley would have a hard time believing it.

Meanwhile, a new apprehension is gnawing at the fringes of Anglo worry about the lessening quality of America's living conditions. The Pacific Coast is assuming the importance long held by the Atlantic Seaboard, and the great metropolis of Los Angeles is becoming the capital of the Third World. Concentrating in it are immigrants from Mexico and Guatemala and other countries south of the Rio Grande, and more and more "New Americans" immigrating from Vietnam, Cambodia, and elsewhere in Southeast Asia. English is a foreign language in many barrios of the city, and Anglo residents fear they themselves may soon become a minority as the Indians became before them.

The objective, illumined, and prophetic counsel of Chief Seattle would almost certainly assure us today that we are now on the threshold of another cyclical change, a new era. This one is not limited to the United States, but is worldwide: the greatest change in the life of mankind since the beginning of the Christian era.

What it will bring no one knows. But we can obtain a glimpse into the future from the immeasurable past of the people who are the oldest inhabitants of America. They have endured through the centuries because of their loving respect for the earth and their sense of unity with all that exists. This may be a lesson the tormented and fragmented world can learn from them before it is too late: to establish relationships and love with one another, and with all other forms of living nature.

Deganawidah, The Peacemaker

IT WAS AN EMPIRE of trees then, of hardwood hickory, elm, and oak, of the slim white birch, balsam, fir, and spruce, all governed by their chief, the lofty pine whose tip seemed to reach the sky: an almost unbroken virgin forest that stretched from the Atlantic to the Mississippi, and from Canada to the Carolinas.

Eight Iroquoian tribes claimed the northern part of the forest from the mouth of the St. Lawrence River to the middle of the Great Lakes. Lake Huron and Lake Erie were named after two of the tribes, and the Mohawk River after a third. The other five tribes were no less important: the Senecas, Oneidas, Cayugas, Onondagas, and Susquehannas. Still another Iroquois tribe, the Tuscaroras in North Carolina, eventually moved north to join the others.

The Peacemaker was born into the Huron tribe before Columbus reached America, at least so long ago that what little contradictory myths and legends tell about him has the dreamlike texture of a fairy tale. This is natural. For The Peacemaker himself had a dream: a wonderful, practical dream that came true for all America.

The Peacemaker's mother and grandmother were very poor, living alone in the forest. According to legend they both were very frightened by his virgin birth and by portents that he would bring evil upon his tribe. Three times they tried to drown the infant in an icy river. Yet on the morning after each attempt he was found safe at home in the arms of his surprised mother.

"Clearly it is decreed that he should live," they agreed, and so they reared him as best they could.

As The Peacemaker grew to manhood he was possessed by the magic power which came from the Great Spirit pervading and uniting all things. The Iroquois name for this mysterious and impersonal force or energy was *orenda*. A man could be inspired to great deeds or enabled to foretell future events by its divine power. It came to him when he fasted and prayed alone in the forest. Most often it came to him through a dream.

So it was with The Peacemaker. During one of his lonely vigils he had a strange dream. Perhaps it was natural that he dreamed of the chief of the forest, the lofty pine. But this pine was stronger and larger than any man had seen. Its roots were the five most powerful tribes of the Iroquois, and its trunk rose so high that its tip pierced through the sky to the Great Spirit of all life. On top sat an eagle watching to see that none of the tribes broke the peace between them.

For days afterward The Peacemaker kept thinking about the meaning of the dream. His village was set in a clearing, surrounded by a stockade of logs. Inside the log houses made of slabs of elm bark, women were sewing fringed buckskin dresses, shirts, leggings, and moccasins. Others outside were tending patches of corn, beans, and squash. Men were skinning a deer. Children were playing. How peaceful it seemed!

Yet all too often this peace was broken by the return of a war party gliding downriver in their canoes, paddles flashing in the sun. Each man was stripped and painted, and all his hair was shaved off except a tuft on the crown, the scalp lock. Usually they brought back a captive, a handsome young warrior like themselves, head erect, a proud look on his face. The Peacemaker knew that war among the Iroquois was not a great tribal undertaking to destroy another tribe and take its land. It was carried on only by small raiding parties of young men to gain fame, and to capture prisoners in order to test their bravery.

One day he watched the torture of such a prisoner.

The captive's first ordeal came when he was forced to run between two lines of Huron warriors who struck him with their clubs and slashed him with their knives as he passed. Afterward, beaten and gashed, he was allowed to rest and given food. Then he was tied to a stake, and a slow fire was lit at his feet.

Iroquois torture was notorious for its prolonged cruelty. Even the women participated, pouring red-hot coals on his head and gouging out bits of his flesh as the fire ate up his legs. To prolong his agony, they let him rest often. The young prisoner was brave, too proud to betray his suffering. He sang, boasted of his own tribe, ridiculed his enemies.

Offered a gourd of water during a short rest, the prisoner replied haughtily, "Drink it yourself! Does not water flow through the veins of a Huron instead of blood?" The torture continued. And not until the following morning did his proud spirit finally leave his mutilated, blackened body.

"What a waste of a life!" thought The Peacemaker. "This constant torturing and warring between tribes must stop. That is what my dream foretold."

He tried to explain his dream of peace to his tribe, but the Hurons would not listen. "There has always been war. It is the custom," they said, interrupting his explanation. Perhaps they could not be blamed. For The Peacemaker stuttered so badly it was difficult to understand him.

Yet filled with the power of *orenda*, he dressed in spotless white buckskin, stepped into a white birchbark canoe, and went in search of someone to speak for him. After many days of paddling over lakes and down streams, ever to the east, he entered the country of the Mohawks. Here, sitting outside a bark lodge deep in the forest, was a man named Hiawatha. They began to talk, Hiawatha patiently listening to The Peacemaker's stuttering description of his dream and his explanation of its meaning.

"And how do you propose to accomplish this Great Peace?" Hiawatha finally asked.

"We are all branches of the one Tree of Life," answered The

Peacemaker. "But we must unite the roots, the five tribes, in a league to establish the peace."

"I understand. Well, let us begin," assented Hiawatha. "As your name means 'Two Rivers Flowing Together,' and mine 'He Makes Rivers,' it is clear that we are meant to work together."

They were a well-matched pair as they traveled from tribe to tribe: Hiawatha, an eloquent orator, explaining the Great Peace to one council after another; and The Peacemaker, a great organizer, developing the form of the league he had in mind. Their pitiless opponent was Hiawatha's half-brother Todadaho, a wizard and the fierce chief of the Onondaga tribe. By the power of his sorcery he killed Hiawatha's wife and three daughters in an attempt to stop their efforts.

Still the two organizers persisted, securing the consent of four tribes to join the league: the Oneidas, Mohawks, Cayugas, and Senecas. Finally the Onondagas assented when The Peacemaker proposed that they be given the privilege of lighting the council fires. Chiefs of these five tribes met in the forest with their assembled councilmen and warriors, establishing the ritual of the founding of the league.

"We now uproot the tallest pine, chief of the forest," proclaimed The Peacemaker through his spokesman Hiawatha. "Into the earth we cast our clubs and hatchets, all our weapons of war, and replant the tree over them." Staring upward toward the tip of the pine which pierced the sky to the spirit of all life, he concluded, "Thus have we established the Great Peace according to my dream. Now let us keep watch, like the eagle above, to see that it is never broken."

So was formed the League of the Iroquois, the Confederation of the Five Nations. Like the Great Tree, it was rooted in symbolism. The five roots, east, south, west, north, and center, were represented by the five tribes or nations. Of these, the Mohawks, Senecas, and Onondagas represented the male side of the League, and the Oneidas and Cayugas the female. The Confederation was thus an organic unity, and it did preserve the peace for two hundred years.

Much later the Tuscaroras joined when they were driven from the south, making it a league of six nations. The failure of The Peace-maker's own Hurons to ally themselves with the League confirmed the prophecies made at the time of his birth. After a disastrous war with the Iroquois Confederation, they migrated west to settle on the Huron River in Ottawa country, becoming known as Wyandots. Later they moved south into the Ohio Valley. The Eries and the Susque-hannas (or Conestogas) also disputed the power of the Iroquois Confederation and were defeated. Large numbers of the Eries were captured and adopted into the Seneca tribe; some Conestogas were driven into Pennsylvania, others adopted by the Oneidas.

By 1570 the Confederation of the Five Nations had developed into an amazing political organization. Before it was formed, government had been exercised by clans which gradually allied to form tribes. The Confederation now allied the large tribes into one governing body, but without destroying the authority of the lowest levels. All power still flowed upward from the people, rather than being enforced by a ruling class above. This was achieved in a novel, democratic way.

A central council was formed of fifty sachems, or chiefs, from all five tribes. They were selected by the mothers of families possessing hereditary chieftainship rights, but were subject to popular vote, male and female, and confirmation by the council. These women exercised the right of initiative, referendum, and recall, probably for the first time in America. A sachem served for life, and the one who replaced him took his name.

The Peacemaker, who formulated these constitutional principles, did not have a mother of such a line of descent, and hence his name as a sachem was not perpetuated. He himself exclaimed, "To others let there be successors, for like them they can advise you. But I have established your commonwealth, and none have done what I have done."

He served on the council with another group of members known as Pine Trees or Pine Tree Chiefs. Any man could earn this title by merit, without regard to hereditary right.

The central council met in the Onondaga country whenever it was necessary to settle a matter affecting all tribes. The Onondagas served as "Keepers of the Fire." Each question was thoroughly debated. One chief after another stood up and spoke at length. When all had voiced their opinions, a vote was taken. Each tribe had one vote. If the vote was not unanimous, the matter was discussed until all tribes were in agreement.

The important aims of the Confederation were to ensure the people's welfare and defense against enemies, to maintain peace between individuals and tribes, and to promote proper conduct and right thought necessary for the maintenance of human rights and justice. Underlying the civil powers necessary to accomplish these aims was the divine power of *orenda*. The Confederation recognized this by creating a separate group in each tribe known as "Keepers of the Faith." They were in charge of the many religious ceremonies held to strengthen the decisions of the council. Almost all of these included dances, for the Iroquois regarded dancing as a form of worship.

Only legend relates what happened to the founders of the League. The Peacemaker, his work done, dressed in white buckskin and paddled away in a luminous white canoe to vanish forever from the sight of men. Hiawatha also disappeared, living on only in the myths and legends of many tribes. From one of these, the Ojibwas, also known as the Chippewas, Longfellow took the name for his poem.

It is enough that in the League of the Iroquois, the Confederation of Five Nations, they established an organic social institution which endured assault by the oncoming white men for two centuries — until the American Revolutionary War split it into factions. In recent years the League of the Iroquois, also known as the Haudenosaunee, has resurfaced and is undergoing a revival. The League is once again openly active, not only within its own tribes, but at national and international levels as well, particularly in areas of sovereignty and human rights.

The influence of the League of the Iroquois upon the course of this nation, the United States of America, has been in the highest degree. For it is believed now that because the framers of the Constitution were familiar with the League, the charter for the government of the United States was modeled upon many of its principles. Whether or not this is true, the symbols of the great pine and the eagle, and the concept of a number of separate peoples united in a federation for the good of all, were derived from American roots and given practical expression through The Peacemaker and Hiawatha.

Powhatan

To the south of the iroquois another confederacy, this one of Algonquian tribes, was formed by a Pamunkey chief named Wahunsonacock.

The Algonquians were an enormous language-family of tribes spread over what is now the Canadian border and the eastern United States. Wahunsonacock's territory lay in Virginia, and in the latter part of the sixteenth century he was able to bring under his control thirty tribes and two hundred villages. His headquarters were at Powhatan, meaning "Falls of the River," located at the falls of the James River and near the present site of Richmond. Thereafter the alliance of the tribes was known as the Powhatan Confederacy, and Wahunsonacock as its ruling chief was called The Powhatan or simply Powhatan.

In 1608, there arrived several shiploads of English colonists who had been sent by a London stock company to gain a foothold in America. Near the mouth of the James River they established Jamestown, the first permanent English colony in North America. Their leader or governor, Captain John Smith, then set forth upriver with a small party toward Pamunkey Creek, where Powhatan lived with the leading tribe of his confederacy.

On January 12 Smith's barge reached the small village of Werawocomoco. The river was partly frozen, and the men were forced to wade waist-deep through the icy ooze. The Indians quartered them in their wigwams and fed them bread, turkey, and venison that Powhatan had sent. They then marched to Powhatan's village.

It was a large compound of wigwams enclosed by a palisade of logs, which housed nearly a thousand people. The wigwams were oblong in shape with rounded roofs made of bent saplings covered with the bark of trees and rush mats to shed the rain. Inside was an open fire, the smoke escaping through a hole in the roof. Powhatan's wigwam was the largest, nearly a hundred feet long. Into this, Captain Smith and his party were ushered and given a royal feast.

Powhatan wore a headdress of feathers and many shell necklaces. He was about sixty years old, with a dignified bearing and a stern face that reflected his rather cranky disposition. Captain John Smith recognized him at once as the "King of Pamunkey" and held forth a copper crown.

"Our sovereign across the great water, the king of England, sends you greeting and his crown," he said.

Powhatan took off his feather headdress and bent his head just an instant to receive the crown, for he did not fancy bowing his head to anyone.

Then the talk began. Two of Captain Smith's company, Walter Russell and Anas Todkill, with the aid of interpreters, recorded it carefully. Captain Smith thanked Powhatan for his turkey and venison, but observed that Powhatan had sent no corn. Powhatan replied that he had little corn to spare, but that he would trade forty measures of corn for forty swords.

Answered Captain Smith:

> As for swords and guns, I have none to spare. And you shall know
> that those I have can keep me from want. Yet steal or wrong you,
> I will not, nor dissolve that friendship we have mutually promised,
> except you constrain me by your bad usage.

Powhatan promised to obtain some corn for him, but expressed fear of the Englishman's purpose:

> Yet some doubt I have of your coming hither, that makes me not
> so kindly seek to relieve you as I would. For many do inform me
> your coming is not for trade, but to invade my people and possess

my country, who do dare not come to bring you corn, seeing you
thus armed with your men. To cheer us of this fear, leave aboard
your weapons. For here they are needless, we being all friends and
forever Powhatans.

Captain Smith, refusing to give up his weapons, spent the night in
Powhatan's palatial wigwam and resumed the talk next day. Insisting
on corn, he managed to obtain ten measures in trade for a copper
kettle. Powhatan, who valued the kettle very highly and was "exceedingly liberal with what he had not," promptly gave Captain Smith a
tract of land called Monacan in promise for more trade goods the
following year.

Captain Smith was satisfied, and Powhatan seemed assured that
a basis of permanent peace had been established. In a long speech
he said:

> Captain Smith, I know the difference between peace and war
> better than anyone else in my country. . . . But that you are said
> to come to destroy my country so much affrights all my people as
> they dare not visit you. . . .
>
> What will it avail you to take that by force which you may
> quietly obtain with love, or to destroy them that provide you with
> food?
>
> Let this therefore assure you of our love, and every year our
> friendly trade shall furnish you with corn. And now also if you
> would come in a friendly manner to see us, and not thus with your
> guns and swords, as to invade your foes.

So was peace established with the Powhatans, and land obtained
for the price of a copper kettle.

Nearly half of the nine hundred Jamestown colonists died of hard-
ships. Without the help of the Powhatans, even the survivors would
have perished. They learned how to erect wigwams until they could
build houses. The Powhatans taught them to fertilize their fields
with seaweed; to plant corn, beans, pumpkins, squash; to bake clams

and a pot of beans in a hole in the ground. The settlers, most of whom had never seen corn, found there were many ways to cook it: boiling the ears in water, roasting them in ashes, making hominy of the kernels, and a stew of corn and beans called *succotash*. For the first time, they smoked that strange native leaf called *tobacco*, and began to use for money the beautiful strings and belts of clamshell beads called *wampum*. Many such Algonquian words the settlers adopted into the English language: *wigwam*, *tomahawk*, *hominy*, *squaw*, and *papoose*.

To replace the colonists who had died, more shiploads were sent by the London stock company which financed the colony. The new arrivals were ordered to make a profit for the stockholders by any means. Instead of clearing new forest land for themselves, they drove Powhatans off their fields, burned their villages, and worked those captured as slaves. The Powhatans fought back, killing colonists and capturing Captain John Smith.

Powhatan from his high seat looked down at the bound prisoner who had been brought before him. He had discarded his English crown for his feather headdress. His face was clouded with anger as he raised his club-shaped tomahawk over Captain Smith's head: "By this you shall receive the punishment you deserve."

At this moment occurred one of the most famous incidents in early American history. According to the romantic version, Powhatan's favorite daughter rushed in, flung herself on Captain Smith's body, and begged for his life. It is probably more true she entered quietly, and as a chief's daughter claimed Captain Smith as her captive, according to Powhatan custom. In any case, Captain Smith's life was spared on the condition that the colonists stop encroaching. He soon returned to England.

Fighting was resumed after he sailed. The new governor, Sir Thomas Dale, had found he could make the company profit by exporting smoking tobacco, which had become fashionable in England. But tobacco quickly wore out the soil, and new fields were needed. So the Indians were driven farther and farther away to make room for great plantations. Powhatan retreated to Werawocomoco. And here he was brought distressing news by a messenger who crouched at his feet, almost afraid to talk.

"My dearest daughter Pocahontas?" exclaimed Powhatan, rising to his feet in wrath. "The Coat-Wearing People will suffer for this! We will kill and kill until we recapture her. Send word to all chiefs!"

"It is too late for that," replied the trembling messenger. "They have taken her to a big ship that our canoes cannot attack. This is what I have come to tell you."

She indeed had been lured on board an English ship in the Potomac and carried to Jamestown as a hostage. Powhatan's anger cooled. Worry ate into him like a worm. He became frantic over his loss.

For this mischievous wisp of a girl always had been the one tender, beautiful flower in the old chief's life. Even as a child she had been more fond than most children of playthings like sea shells and little wampum beads. Lighthearted and gay, she was always laughing and seeking amusement. Hence Powhatan had named her Matoaka, "One Who Amuses Herself." As she grew into a dusky-skinned young maiden, her amazing pranks completely befuddled her stern father. He took to calling her Pocahontas, "Playful." She was, in fact, a spoiled teenager to whom he could refuse nothing.

And now she was held captive by the English. "Why?" he asked himself. As days of torment and sleepless nights passed, he began to suspect the reason. The English were holding her hostage in order to demand a huge ransom for her release. Powhatan already had ordered his warriors to stop fighting lest her life be endangered. "What more will the English demand?" he questioned. "That my people give up their homes and move from our beloved tidelands?" And now he was torn between love for his daughter and his people. Unable to decide, he relapsed into a black melancholy out of which he would erupt in a burst of anger.

Eventually a message was brought him from the tyrannical governor of the Jamestown Colony, Sir Thomas Dale. It could not have been worse. Pocahontas wanted to adopt Christianity and marry one of the colony's largest tobacco planters, John Rolfe. Like most fathers of spoiled daughters, Powhatan was stunned. Certainly she had been fascinated from her first sight of these light-skinned, bearded men dressed in beautiful clothes. Perhaps it was this attraction that had impelled her to save the life of Captain John Smith, even though she was married to Kocoum, one of Powhatan's warriors. But for her to marry an Englishman was something he could not understand.

Escorted to Jamestown, Powhatan was taken to his capricious seventeen-year-old daughter. "Pocahontas! My dearest daughter!" Was it she or not? She was dressed in silk and satin, with shoes on her feet. But more than her new clothes, it was her new manner that confused him. She was no longer playful and amusing, but composed and quietly smiling.

"Is this what you wish? To marry a Coat-Wearing Man? One who is stealing our land to plant tobacco on it? Are you sure you're not being tricked?"

To all his anxious questions, Pocahontas gave one grave answer: "It is what I want."

If Powhatan was mystified, Sir Thomas Dale also wondered why John Rolfe, an honest gentleman and of good behavior, wanted to marry an illiterate, pagan Indian girl. To clear the governor's doubts, John Rolfe wrote him a long letter:

> Let therefore this my well advised protestation, which here I make between God and my own conscience, be sufficient witness at the dreadful day of judgement . . . if my chiefest intent and purpose be . . . in no way led (so far forth as man's weakness may permit) with the unbridled desire of carnal affection; but the good of this plantation, for the honor of our country, for the glory of God, for my own salvation, and for the converting to the true knowledge of God and Jesus Christ, an unbelieving creature, namely Pocahontas. To whom my heart and best thoughts are, and have a long

time been so entangled, and enthralled in so intricate a labyrinth. . . .

So in this intricate labyrinth of motives and emotions Pocahontas and John Rolfe were married in April 1614. Soon afterward they sailed for England with Sir Thomas Dale and Pocahontas's brother-in-law Uttomatomac. The marriage proved indeed to be for the good of the plantation. Powhatan stopped fighting and kept peace with the colonists.

In London John Rolfe presented Pocahontas under her baptismal name of Lady Rebecca to Queen Anne, introduced her to the famous Ben Jonson, and gave her all the luxury a bride could wish. She gave birth to a son, Thomas Rolfe. Soon afterward her portrait was painted by an artist at court. It showed her arrayed in an embroidered velvet gown with a lace ruff around the throat, wearing white gloves and a tiny black hat, and holding a fan. Very fashionable indeed! Yet out of this finery there looked the pathetic face of a simple Indian girl of twenty-one, suffering from the cold dampness of England, and pining for her carefree, playful life in her native land. A year later, just three years after her marriage, she died of smallpox.

Powhatan died the following year, 1618, a disillusioned old man. Tobacco was making enormous profits for the English company, and its planters were taking more land for the development of great plantations.

Opechancanough replaced Powhatan as chief of the Powhatan Confederacy. A deadly foe of the whites, he launched a general uprising against the colonists in 1622. Every settlement except Jamestown was attacked, and 347 colonists were killed. The English retaliated with a campaign to exterminate every Indian man, woman, and child in all Virginia. All troop commanders were forbidden to make peace upon any terms whatever. Opechancanough was killed and his head cut off. Only a few survivors were left to carry on a sporadic resistance.

Years later Pocahontas's son, Thomas Rolfe, returned to his mother's homeland. He became a wealthy tobacco planter and founded one of Virginia's most aristocratic families. Its descendants today can be proud of a lineage that stems back to the mischievous daughter of the chief of the once great Powhatan Confederacy.

Among the few memorials to Pocahontas today is a statue of her that stands in the churchyard at Gravesend, England, on the River Thames below London, where she was buried in 1617. Her exact burial site at the church is unknown.

Massasoit & Metacomet

BETWEEN THE IROQUOIS TO THE NORTH and the Powhatans to the south were a number of small tribes occupying the coast of southern New England. It was to one of these, the Wampanoags, that a ship hove into sight on December 21, 1620.

The ship did not justify her name of the sweet *Mayflower*. She was a rank old tub of 180 tons which for years had hauled fish, turpentine, and other smelly products from Norway. In her dark, nauseous quarters below deck were crowded 102 passengers, all "from the cottages and not the castles of England." They were the vanguard of English colonists called Puritans because they preached a frighteningly strict religion, and Pilgrims because they had separated from the Church of England and pilgrimaged to this new land to practice what they preached.

Through the falling snow the shivering Wampanoags watched the exploring party row ashore to a rocky point called Plymouth. Seeing the Indians, one of the Pilgrim Fathers shot off his musket. The Wampanoags fled back into the woods. The exploring party marched inland, discovering much land that had been cleared and planted to corn several years before, a hill commanding the harbor, and a "very sweete brooke with much good fishe." Here along the brook on the southern shore of the harbor, the Pilgrims established their colony of New Plymouth.

Work began at once: laying out a street along Town Brook to Fort Hill, on which Captain Miles Standish mounted his cannon; planning a Common House; and staking off lots for every member of the colony. More Indians kept appearing. Finally a tall, powerful warrior strode across the clearing to the Common House. He was naked save for a deerskin breechclout, and was carrying a bow and arrows. The Pilgrims, embarrassed by his nakedness, hurriedly threw about him a red horseman's coat. Then the talk began.

The warrior, Samoset, could speak a little English. He lived up the coast, where he was chief of the Abenakis, or Wabenakis. "Free in speeche, so farr as he could expresse his mind," he told the Pilgrims the Indian name for New Plymouth was Patuxet, meaning "Little Bay." Three years before, the "plague," probably smallpox, had wiped out the Patuxet tribe, accounting for the abandoned cornfields. The chief of all tribes in the region was Samoset's friend, sachem of the Wampanoags who lived not so far to the southwest. His name was Cusamequin, "Yellow Feather," better known as Massasoit.

A few days later Samoset returned with a friend named Squanto, who could speak excellent English. The news they brought was exciting: the great chief Massasoit was on his way to visit the white men. Soon Massasoit appeared with sixty warriors whose faces were painted black, red, yellow, or white. Massasoit's own face was painted "a sad mulberry." He wore a deerskin robe and a great chain of white beads to which were fastened a long knife and a leather tobacco pouch. He was solemn and dignified, grave in mien and manner.

Leaving their bows and arrows behind, the Wampanoags were saluted by a squad of Pilgrim musketeers and escorted to Governor John Carver, Edward Winslow, and other Pilgrim Fathers. The chief was presented with a pair of knives, a copper chain, biscuits, and a "Pot of Strong Water." Then with Squanto and Samoset as interpreters, the governor and Massasoit pledged themselves not to "doe hurte" to one another in any way, the pact applying to all tribes under Massasoit. This memorable peace treaty was never broken by the Wampanoags until Massasoit's death forty years later.

The colonists were badly in need of help. Not knowing how to build log cabins, they erected houses of wattle and daub with steep thatched roofs. These flimsy cottages were too cold to live in, so the people remained on board the *Mayflower* until the ship sailed early in April. In their cramped and unsanitary quarters they were afflicted by the "General Sickness" — a combination of scurvy, pneumonia, and tuberculosis — which killed off half the company, including Governor Carver. Without Squanto and Massasoit's men, the survivors would have also perished.

Squanto showed them how to plant corn in hillocks, first placing three herrings spoke-wise to fertilize the earth, and how to build traps in the stream to catch fish; and he also acted as a guide and an interpreter. Perplexed by his fluent English, the colonists said to him, "Exceedingly strange we find ye English language on your tongue."

Squanto explained how he had learned the language. Several years before, he and twenty Patuxet warriors had been captured by an English exploring party, carried to Spain, and sold in the slave market at Malaga. A Christian friar then had slipped Squanto into England to work for a rich merchant. Finally obtaining passage on a trading ship, Squanto was set ashore on the New England coast and eventually made his way home. Here he found that pestilence had carried off all his tribe, leaving him the last of the Patuxets. He had then gone to live with the Wampanoags.

The Pilgrims did not doubt that Squanto was "a speciall instrumente sent of God for their good beyond their expectation."

That October the Pilgrims held a day of thanksgiving for all the blessings they had enjoyed. Their English wheat, barley, and peas had not grown, but the twenty acres of Indian corn Squanto had planted for them gave a good crop. Due to Massasoit's friendship they walked "as peaceably and safely in the woods as in the highways in England." Seven homes and four buildings for common use now lined the street of New Plymouth.

On the day of the harvest festival Massasoit arrived with ninety warriors. With them they brought deer, geese, duck, and "turkies," clams and eels, with wild plums, dried berries, and "sallet herbes." The first harvest festival celebrated by the English immigrants was such a success it was held every October thereafter until President Lincoln in 1863 proclaimed it a national holiday, designating the last Thursday in November as Thanksgiving Day.

During the following years more colonists arrived, establishing trading posts from Maine to Connecticut. The focus of settlement was to the north, around Massachusetts Bay. Here bands of Puritans, carrying a Breeches Bible in one hand and a musket in the other, rapidly founded many prosperous towns: Boston, Salem, Water-town, Lynn, and Roxbury. Along all the coast thousands of more settlers were pouring in, not only English, but Dutch and Swedish. Land was needed for homes and towns, to grow corn and to raise cattle. The settlers bought it from the Indians or simply drove them off their homelands.

Thousands of acres were distributed to members of the Plymouth Colony. Noble old Massasoit, faithful to his treaty, gave away a large tract around the town of Swansea to the Pilgrims on the condition that they would not attempt to draw his people away from their own religion. Trouble began when the Wampanoags continued to hunt and fish on land they had sold, and were arrested and convicted of trespassing.

Captain Miles Standish and two companions obtained a tract fourteen miles square near Bridgewater. "Did we not buy this for seven coats, eight hoes, nine hatchets, ten yards of cotton cloth, twenty knives, and four moose skins?" they demanded in court. "Now it is ours. No one has the right to trespass upon our property."

Massasoit tried to defend the trespassers: "What is this you call property? It cannot be the earth. For the land is our Mother, nourishing all her children, beasts, birds, fish, and all men. The woods, the streams, everything on it belongs to everybody and is for the use of all. How then can one man say it belongs to him only?"

"Why did you sell us this land then?"

"Because you are strangers far from your own earth, we sold you only the right to use the land also."

It was no use arguing. The Indians could not understand the European concept of land titles to private property with exclusive use by the owners. Nor could the whites understand the Indian conception of general use of the land. The English attitude was clearly expressed at a town meeting: "Voted, that the earth is the Lord's and the fulness thereof; voted, that the earth is given to the Saints; voted, that we are the Saints."

They continued to appropriate Indian land.

The "Saints on the Bay," as the Massachusetts Bay Puritans were called, were further infuriated by the refusal of the Wampanoags, Pequots, Narragansets, and Nipmucks to accept Christianity. Massasoit still counseled peace, and sent his two sons to the colonists' school. Wamsutta, the elder son, the colonists renamed Alexander; and Metacomet, the younger, Philip. The boys grew up in an atmosphere of increasing tension. It was suddenly broken when the Massachusetts Bay Puritans under Captain John Mason attacked a Pequot village near the mouth of the Mystic River in Connecticut, set it afire, and massacred most of its seven hundred inhabitants as they tried to escape the flames.

It was a fearful sight, reported the Reverend Cotton Mather, "to see them thus frying in ye fyer, and ye streams of blood quenching ye same, and horrible was ye stinck and sente thereof; but ye victory seemed a sweete sacrifice, and they gave prayse thereof to God." Of the few prisoners taken, the men were sold into slavery in the West Indies, and the women divided among the soldiers.

Metacomet was horrified and perplexed. "Look, here is a picture of the seal of the Massachusetts Bay Colony," he said to his father. "See the Indian on it? I will read you the words coming out of his mouth: 'Come over and help us.' That is what these Puritans teach. But look how they practice it! The Pequot Nation is no more. Those who are left are forbidden to call themselves Pequot!"

"The Puritans are our friends," stubbornly insisted Massasoit.

When noble old Massasoit died in 1661, a friend of the English to the end, trouble no longer could be averted. Wamsutta, or Alexander, named chief, was seized and taken to the governor on charges of plotting against Pilgrims. Finally released, he died at Plymouth a few days later of fever and "inward fury." Metacomet, whom the English now called Philip of Pokanoket or King Philip, succeeded him as chief of the Wampanoags.

More and more restrictions were put upon him. He was forced to acknowledge himself not only a subject of the Crown but of the "government of New Plymouth." The pledge was exacted of him: "I doe promise not to dispose of any of the lands I have at presente but by the approbation of the Governour of Plimouth." And finally he was made to pay an indemnity of £100 and a yearly tribute of five wolves' heads.

"Keep paying tribute," he counseled his warriors. "We are but buying time to get ready."

He began secretly organizing his fighting men in the forests, and obtaining muskets for them. One by one he went to the Nipmucks, Sakonnets, Pocassets, Nausets, Pamets, and other tribes to enlist their support. A small group of Mohegans and "Praying Indians" who had adopted Christianity refused. But Canonchet, chief of the powerful Narraganset tribe, welcomed him warmly. They agreed to begin an organized war in the spring of 1676.

But early in 1675, when a settler shot an Indian for trespassing on his land, there began the uprising known as King Philip's War. It was fought with fanatical fury on both sides. Philip, like a phantom in the forests, deployed his forces with skill and cunning. As tribe after tribe joined him, he struck at Dartmouth, Taunton, Scituate.

Panic spread throughout Massachusetts, Rhode Island, and Connecticut. A large English army was raised, each town being made responsible for recruiting soldiers. Any able-bodied man refusing to serve was fined or compelled to run the gauntlet. They were urged on by Puritan ministers in their pulpits exhorting them to exterminate the savage Canaanites who had dared to attack "the whole nation, yea the whole Israel of God." Even the "Praying Indians" were driven from their villages, placed in confinement, and put to death on the slightest suspicion.

King Philip continued to attack and burn towns — Lancaster, Medfield, Weymouth, Marlborough. His military genius was apparent: of the ninety English towns, he attacked fifty-two, completely destroying twelve of them. The English army was ruthless. Marching on the Narragansets assembled in the Great Swamp near Kingston, Rhode Island, on a winter Sabbath morning, the soldiers slaughtered hundreds of men, women, and children. Chief Canonchet was captured and promptly executed by being drawn and quartered.

King Philip's wife and nine-year-old son were then captured. "My heart breaks!" he cried upon hearing the news. "Now I am ready to die!"

Announced the Reverend Cotton Mather in Boston: "It must be as bitter as death for him to lose his wife and only son, for the Indians are marvelously fond and affectionate towards their children."

By the summer of 1676 the tide of the battle had turned against King Philip. His forces, retreating into the forests and swamps, without food, and becoming weak and diseased, began to desert him. He himself was finally killed in a swamp. His head was cut off and carried triumphantly to Plymouth, his hands being sent to Boston. The rest of his body was quartered and left to the wolves.

The war was over. All the Wampanoag lands were seized and sold. The victorious English colonists swarmed over the land, hunting down fleeing Indian men, women, and children, and selling them as slaves. Some five hundred were shipped to the West Indies from Plymouth alone. Among these were King Philip's wife and son.

The citizens of Plymouth mounted King Philip's head on a pole set on Fort Hill. Reverend Mather later carried away as a trophy the jawbone of "that blasphemous leviathan." Thereafter for twenty years the surviving portion of the head remained on the pole — the bleaching skull of the Wampanoags' greatest war leader, son of the noble Massasoit who had helped the Pilgrim Fathers to establish here their first colony in New England.

A 19th century historian, Samuel Drake, wrote of Massasoit, "He was a chief renowned more in peace than war, and was as long as he lived, a friend to the English, notwithstanding they committed repeated usurpations upon his lands and liberties."

Of his son, King Philip, 19th century historian William Weeden wrote, "He almost made himself a king by his marvelous energy and statecraft put forth among the New England tribes. Had the opposing power been a little weaker, he might have founded a temporary kingdom on the ashes of the colonies."

Pontiac

PONTIAC WAS A MAN OF STEEL pounded between a British hammer and a French anvil. Early on that July morning in 1755 when he was about to be caught between them, he sat staring at the log stockade surrounding Fort Duquesne. It stood where Pittsburgh now stands, at the strategic spot where the Allegheny and Monongahela rivers join to form the great Ohio. Pontiac was thirty-five years old, of medium build, with an unusually dark complexion and a bold and stern expression. A man of strong will, he was used to being obeyed and had never been known to break his own word. Whenever he wanted to buy anything, he would issue a promissory note drawn upon a slab of birchbark and signed with the figure of an otter, his totem animal. It was always faithfully redeemed.

The problem he now confronted was one of allegiance. The year before, a small English party had begun to build a fort here. Then a flotilla of French and Indians came downriver in three hundred canoes. They drove off the English and took over the fort, naming it Duquesne. Now a big English army was coming to take it back. The fort commander was considering retreat when Beaujeu, one of his captains, boldly proposed enlisting Ottawas, Ojibwas, Hurons, and Delawares to save the fort. Pontiac was named as the leading chief.

"Shall I ally myself with the English or the French?" he asked himself. White men were white men. But still he had observed some differences. The French were trappers, *coureurs de bois*. And this country of both his parents, an Ottawa chief and Ojibwa mother, was superb trapping country, especially for beaver. With its lakes, rivers, and countless small waterways, it also supplied fish in abundance. There was no need to farm. The Indians had a bountiful supply of grain they didn't need to cultivate at all — wild rice. The French called it *avoine folle*, "crazy oats." To gather it, Ojibwas had only to bend the tall stalks over their canoes and knock off the grain with small wooden paddles.

The French voyageurs and fur traders fitted naturally into the life of the country. They learned to travel miles on snowshoes, and paddle thirty-foot-long birchbark canoes with skill. For fur they traded the Indians excellent hatchets, knives, kettles, and guns. Jolly men, they sang while they worked. They learned the language. And they often married Ottawa and Ojibwa girls. No wonder they had secured such a strong foothold in the wilderness. The French controlled all of Canada and the Great Lakes country, and were establishing posts down the Mississippi Valley all the way to their big colony at New Orleans.

The English, thought Pontiac, were dour and greedy. They cheated Indians. And regarding themselves as superior, they seldom intermarried into the tribes. But they were a powerful people. They dominated the Atlantic Seaboard from New England to Virginia, and were now pushing their settlement into the Upper Ohio Valley. Which of them, the French or the English, was to control the valley and open it to settlement? Pontiac intended to be on the winning side in order to ensure peace for his people and a ready sale of furs. But of course it was a choice between two evils. Win or lose, the Indians were certain to lose to the advancing white men.

The problem, big as it seemed to the Ottawa chief sitting alone on a summer morning, was bigger than he knew. In far-off Europe a war was beginning with Austria, France, Sweden, and Russia on one side, and England and Prussia on the other, that was to last till 1763. The French and Indian War, which started in 1754, was but the American phase of the larger war in Europe. The big issue it would decide was whether France or England was to dominate the whole New World and its rich resources.

Pontiac's reveries were broken by the sudden booming of guns at the fort. He could see Beaujeu throwing open the big gates, faintly hear him shouting, "The English are coming!" And now the whole place was swarming with Indian warriors. Pontiac jumped up and swiftly walked up to the fort.

For a month the large English army of thirteen hundred men had been hacking its way through the virgin forest from Fort Cumberland, Virginia. Its commander was Major General Edward Braddock, who had been sent from England to assume command of all British forces in America. He had the reputation of being a military bigot, arrogant and perverse, but a man of personal courage. He had served in Holland under the Prince of Orange, marching out on the battlefield with colors flying and bugles sounding. This plodding through dense, tangled forest was not to Braddock's taste. Daily he grew more irritable.

Then a young Virginian in his column named George Washington came to him: "Sir, our progress is too tedious. May I have your permission to advance with a military escort and a detachment of a hundred axemen to hew a passage for the heavy supply and baggage wagons?"

"Proceed at once!" General Braddock ordered.

The column advanced more rapidly now, but progress was still difficult. Horses strained to drag the ponderous wagons over stumps and roots, and through dense brush. The imported British regiments, sweating in their scarlet uniforms, were oppressed by the gloom of the silent forest. At last, on July 9, the army reached the Monongahela, only nine miles from Fort Duquesne, and began to ford the shallow river.

On the other side, hidden in two ravines, Beaujeu was waiting with a party of French and Canadians, and a horde of Ottawa warriors under Pontiac, aided by Hurons and Ojibwas. There sounded at high noon a single piercing cry. Then a bedlam of war whoops as the attack began. The British soldiers were thrown into panic. One after another fell as they scurried for safety behind trees that hid still more warriors.

Braddock galloped up and down, cursing and shouting, "Form platoons!" The troops huddled together in the forest road like flocks of red-coated sheep, only to be mowed down. Braddock, after having had five horses shot under him, was mortally wounded. Washington could not stop the rout. The men loaded the dying general in a carriage and fled back toward Philadelphia. Of thirteen hundred soldiers, nearly eight hundred had been killed or wounded. Abandoned cannon, baggage, provisions, and wagons were strewn for miles behind them.

Pontiac had saved Fort Duquesne for the French. But not for long. The French forces in the New World were defeated at Quebec, and France in 1763 finally surrendered all Canada to England. Fort Duquesne was turned over to the British, who renamed it Fort Pitt. Other forts fell: Le Boeuf, Presque Isle, Venango. Other western posts still remained to be occupied: Detroit, Michilimackinac, Sault Saint Marie, Quantanon, Miami, Green Bay, and Saint Joseph. Meanwhile, a young adventurer was sent out with a force of two hundred men in canoes to receive the surrender of the French in the name of His Britannic Majesty.

Major Robert Rogers and his Rangers were famous for their marches and adventures, skirmishes and battles. Daring, versed in woodcraft, they knew the wilderness like the Indians themselves. In November they reached the southern margin of Lake Erie, the farthest west that the cross of St. George had ever been carried. But here they were blocked by a large force of Pontiac's warriors.

Rogers demanded to see their chief. Pontiac kept him waiting all day, then strutted in with haughty questions: "What are you doing in my country? How dare you enter it without my permission?"

"The French have been defeated. Canada has surrendered," answered Rogers. "I am now sent to take possession of all French forts and restore peace to white men and Indians."

"The French have surrendered. We Indians have not," Pontiac replied proudly. "If it is to be war to the end between us, let it begin now. My warriors are waiting. If it is to be peace, then let your king, Uncle George, promise to treat my people with respect."

After four days of talk, Rogers agreed to Pontiac's terms. Pontiac not only let him pass unmolested, but restrained the Indians around Detroit from attacking him. Rogers presented his papers to the commandant. The fleur-de-lis was lowered from the flagstaff and the cross of St. George hoisted in its place, while seven hundred Indians watched the transfer of power. Officers were then dispatched to accept the surrender of all other French forts.

Pontiac always had loved this post, founded by de la Mothe Cadillac. Detroit was now a settlement of twenty-five hundred people. In its center was the fort itself, consisting of about a hundred small houses and barracks surrounded by a palisade, with a blockhouse over each gate. Here lived the garrison of 120 soldiers and 40 fur traders. Above and below the fort were strung out the little Canadian houses with their gardens and orchards. On the western shore of the river stood the wigwams of the Potawatomis. On the eastern side rose the Wyandot village. And a few arrow flights above it lay Pontiac's village of Ottawas.

Pontiac himself lived with his wife and children upon a small island at the opening of Lake St. Clair. His home was a wigwam of bark and rushes lined with bearskins. As chief of the loose confederacy of the Ottawas, Ojibwas, and Potawatomis, he was influential among the Illinois tribes and those far down the Ohio. Now, having made terms with Rogers, he looked forward to a prosperous trade with the British.

Unfortunately, Rogers left; and relations between the British and the Indians grew steadily worse. The fur traders cheated and plundered the Indians. Warriors lounging in the fort were cursed and kicked by the soldiers. Resentment kept spreading among the farther tribes as settlements advanced. Pontiac could stand no more insults.

Bearing the war belt of red wampum, he traveled to tribes from Lake Ontario to the Senecas of the Iroquois Confederation, and far southward down the Mississippi. To all of the sachems at council he delivered his message: "The English are coming. Like the waves of the sea they rolled in upon our brothers on the coast. Now they are rolling toward us. Will you be drowned like trapped muskrats? Or will you fight for your homes? The French will help us!"

By the spring of 1763 his plans for a general uprising had been accepted. On May 9 every tribe — Ottawa, Delaware, Huron, Shawnee, and Seneca — was to attack the English fort nearest to it. When all forts had been destroyed, the tribes were to unite in the destruction of all settlements.

"I myself will capture Detroit!" Pontiac promised.

On the night of May 6, an Ojibwa girl named Catherine, who had fallen in love with Gladwyn, commander of the fort, came to see him.

"Tomorrow Pontiac with sixty of his chiefs will come to the fort," she confided. "Each will carry a gun hidden under his blanket. Pontiac will offer you a peace belt of wampum upside down. This will be the signal for the attack. The chiefs will kill you and your officers. The Indians outside will attack the garrison."

Next morning when Pontiac and his chiefs entered the fort, he knew he had been betrayed. On every side stood armed soldiers and fur traders. With an impassive face he strode to Gladwyn waiting in the council house. "Why do I see so many soldiers standing in the street with their guns cocked?" he demanded.

"I have but ordered them under arms for discipline," replied Gladwyn. After a short talk he allowed the chiefs to leave, believing he had taught Pontiac a lesson.

Two days later Pontiac with his Ottawas, Wyandots, Potawatomis, and Ojibwas laid siege to the fort. The same day, on schedule, all the tribes elsewhere swarmed to attack — at Quantanon, Michilimackinac, Niagara, Presque Isle, Le Boeuf, Venango. Of the twelve British posts, eight were captured and their garrisons massacred. Pontiac did not know it then, but his supreme effort to save his country from English invaders had reached its climax. He continued to blockade the fort month after month, and wrote the French to send him help from their posts down the Mississippi.

Late in October disastrous news reached him in a letter from M. Neyon de Villiers, French commander of Fort de Chartres in Louisiana.

France had signed a peace treaty in Paris that February relinquishing not only Canada but all her claims to the land east of the Mississippi. Quite casually M. Neyon mentioned that the defeated French had not forgotten their children and would help them from across the Mississippi. "Now," he concluded, "the Ottawas must live in peace."

With all hope gone that the French could aid him, Pontiac immediately continued to block Detroit. Winter wore on, and then spring. Finally, in August 1764, Captain James Dalyell brought help to the fort after its fifteen-month siege. He himself was killed, but Detroit was saved.

Pontiac watched his Huron, Ojibwa, Delaware, and Seneca allies drift away. Disillusioned but not defeated, he traveled south along the Maumee River and spent the rest of the year trying to enlist Kickapoos, Illinois, and Miamis in a new alliance. The following spring an English detachment sent from Vincennes, Indiana, convinced him his cause was lost; the tribes had given their allegiance to the Crown. Pontiac returned to Detroit and sent a peace pipe to Sir William Johnson, the English government's superintendent of Indian affairs in America.

A year later, heading a delegation of Ottawa, Potawatomi, and Ojibwa chiefs, and accompanied by an English representative from the fort, Pontiac traveled to Johnson Hall at Oswego, New York, and formally sealed his submission to the Crown before Sir William Johnson.

Pontiac's defeat threw open the rich valley of the Ohio to the English. Wandering forlornly through the settlements, he watched more and more huge, cumbersome, canvas-topped wagons rolling in from across Pennsylvania. The settlers called these prairie schooners "Conestogas," a common name for one of the tribes, the Susquehanna, which once had occupied Pennsylvania. There were few of the people left. Pennsylvania was offering bounties of $150 for every captured Indian over ten years old; $134 for every scalp of a killed Indian; $130 for each captured woman or boy under ten years of age; and $50 for the scalp of every slain Indian woman.

In the spring of 1769, just three years after his surrender, Pontiac was murdered at Cahokia, Illinois. The most reliable account is that he was stabbed in the back by a Kaskaskia Indian who had been bribed with a barrel of whiskey by an English trader named Williamson.

Today Pontiac, Michigan, a few arrow flights north of Detroit, is named for this great patriot, who once lived nearby on Apple Island in Orchard Lake.

Thayendanegea,
or Joseph Brant

THAT LOFTIEST OF ALL PINES in the forest, whose roots were the five most powerful tribes of the Iroquois, and whose tip pierced the sky to the spirit of all life. The symbol of the Great Peace, of the League of the Iroquois, the Confederation of the Five Nations. For two hundred winters it had remained unshaken. But now a mighty wind was blowing across the great water from Europe, tearing its roots from the ground.

It had seemed impossible that it could be uprooted. Every year the old sachems and Pine Trees on the council observed the sacred ceremony of the founding of the League. "You see the footprints of our forefathers," they recited. "All but perceptible is the smoke where they used to smoke the pipe together." And they related the deed that had made them great.

In these two centuries the Five Nations had held together like an unbreakable string of beads stretching from east to west: Mohawks, Oneidas, Onondagas, Cayugas, and Senecas. They had brought under their control the Hurons to the north and the Susquehannas, or Conestogas, to the south. When the Tuscaroras had been driven out of North Carolina by the English, the League had given them land and a place in its council, making it a League of Six Nations. Dominating the country from the St. Lawrence out to the Great Lakes, the League had become the most powerful organization of Indians in the United States.

Young Thayendanegea listened carefully to all the stories and counsels of the old men. He was a Mohawk of the Wolf Clan, destined to become a Pine Tree Chief. Moreover, hostilities between the English and the French were leading to the French and Indian War, and it was thought necessary for him to try to understand the position of the League.

"The Ottawas, Ojibwas, and Hurons to the west are helping the French. Are we going to help them or the English?" he asked his father, Tehowaghwengaraghkwin.

"We are our own masters! We cannot be bribed to fight by anyone! Though to be sure, both French and English have tried," his father answered. "Ask Hendrick."

Old "King" Hendrick was the most famous Pine Tree of the Mohawks, even though his father had been Mohegan. He was a fierce-looking old man who often showed Thayendanegea a long line of crosses he had carved on the trunk of a tree. Each cross represented an enemy he had killed or captured. "You've heard that story before," he answered crossly. "It was true. I was one of the four Iroquois councilors taken by the English to visit their Queen. Your grandfather, of course, was another. The Queen called us the Four Kings. She made a man paint a picture of each of us. She gave us presents. All because the English wanted the Iroquois to fight for them. Pagh! We could not be bribed!"

"It is a delicate game we of the League are playing in remaining neutral," concluded Thayendanegea's father. "The wind of war is blowing from both sides. I fear greatly what will happen."

He never lived to see it. Shortly after his death, Thayendanegea's mother married a Mohawk known to the white people as Brant. Thereafter the boy Thayendanegea was called Joseph Brant. And now he met the man who was to change the course of his life.

William Johnson had been sent to America to take charge of a large tract of land in New York for his uncle, Sir Peter Warren. Settling in the Mohawk Valley, Johnson became a prosperous fur trader and built a huge manor house called Johnson Hall. His love affairs were well known to the Mohawks. A young Dutch girl, who had borne him three children, he married on her deathbed. He then had taken to wife a Mohawk girl. And now he married another, Molly Brant, Joseph's older sister.

Joseph liked this bluff and stormy Irishman. He was tall and strong, danced with Mohawk warriors, and harangued the sachems with equal eloquence — just the kind of man who would appeal to a boy. Moreover, he had just been commissioned a major general in the British forces.

With the outbreak of the French and Indian War, Johnson appeared before the council of the League. Flinging down a red wampum belt before the members with a grand gesture, he made a stirring speech asking for Iroquois volunteers. In vain the old sachems pleaded to keep the neutrality of the League. Some two hundred Iroquois answered Johnson's call. Even old "King" Hendrick stepped forward, eager to add a few crosses to the thirty-nine he had carved on his tree. Right behind him was Joseph Brant. "I want to go too!"

Hendrick turned around. "Well! We are both Mohawks and warriors, are we not?"

So the seventy-year-old man and the thirteen-year-old boy marched off with Johnson's English command to fight Baron Dieskau's French forces at Lake George. When they were within a few miles of the French camp, Johnson decided to send a detachment of a thousand men to reconnoiter.

"If they are to be killed, they are too many," protested old Hendrick. "And if they are to fight, they are too few."

Nevertheless, keeping Joseph with him, Johnson ordered out Hendrick with the detachment. The great old Pine Tree Chief never came back to mark another cross on his tree. The detachment was ambushed, almost every man killed. Johnson's main force later defeated the French. And for his diplomatic feat of securing Iroquois volunteers, Colonel Johnson was made a baronet — Sir William Johnson — and awarded £5,000 from the king.

Joseph Brant was a boy of contradictory natures, gentle as a pet coon, savage as a wolf. His first taste of war had awakened his Iroquois ferocity. Now the opposite side of his nature came out when Sir William sent him to the Indian Charity School in Lebanon, Connecticut — which was later moved to New Hampshire and became Dartmouth College. How difficult it was to accustom himself to new clothes and manners, to learn to speak and write English! But Reverend Eleazer Wheelock was an exacting taskmaster, and Joseph was a brilliant pupil. He soaked up book-learning like a sponge and adopted Christianity. While Pontiac to the west was holding the British back from Illinois, Joseph Brant was learning history and devoutly translating the Anglican prayer book and the Acts of the Apostles into Mohawk.

Finishing school, he returned to the Mohawk Valley and became secretary to Sir William Johnson. The baronet, richer than ever, was aging rapidly under the threat of war between the American colonies and their mother country. Turning over his post of superintendent of Indian affairs to his nephew, Guy Johnson, Sir William kept brooding. "Do I owe my and my allies' loyalty to the sovereign who has given me so many honors, or to the land which has enriched me?" he kept asking Joseph Brant. He died in 1774 without making a decision.

It was Joseph Brant who made the decision. In November of 1775 he sailed for England with Colonel Guy Johnson. Brant was now a mature man of diverse talents. As a Pine Tree Chief of the Iroquois, he wore knee-high moccasins and a blanket draped over one shoulder. And as Colonel Guy Johnson's secretary, he was equally at home in starched linen and broadcloth.

What a stir he made in court, this handsome Mohawk chief so suave and polished! He was taken to tea with the famous Boswell, and sat to have his portrait painted by the fashionable artist Romney. Then he got down to business, delivering a speech before Lord George Germaine, secretary of state, and other influential men:

> Brother, we have crossed the great lake and come to this kingdom

with our superintendent, Colonel Johnson, from our Confederacy of the Six Nations and their allies, that we might see our father, the great king, and join in informing him, his counselors, and wise men, of the good intentions of the Indians, and of their attachment to His Majesty and his government. . . .

Brother, the Mohawks, our particular nation, have on all occasions shown their zeal and loyalty to the great king; yet they have been very badly treated by the people in that country, the city of Albany laying an unjust claim to their lands. . . .

We have only, therefore, to request that His Majesty will attend to this matter: it troubles our great nation and they cannot sleep easy in their beds. Indeed it is very hard, when we have let the king's subjects have so much land for so little, they should want to cheat us in this manner of the small spots we have left for our women and children to live on. We are tired out in making complaints and getting no redress. We therefore hope that the assurances now given us by the superintendent may take place and that he may have it in his power to procure justice.

At the end of Brant's long speech, one of the men at the table nodded. "The Mohawks want returned the lands they have lost on the Mohawk and Susquehanna rivers. But this revolution of the thirteen colonies of the Crown is serious. The affray last June on Charleston Heights, above Boston — Bunker Hill, I believe they call it. Very nasty. Yes, it means war. Will the Six Nations serve as our allies?"

The meeting concluded with the agreement that the Mohawks' lands would be restored if the Six Nations would support the British government in its war against the American colonies.

Returning to America, Brant split the Iroquois League wide open by persuading the Mohawks, Senecas, Cayugas, and Onondagas to enlist with the British. The Oneidas and most of the Tuscaroras joined the American forces.

Brant's own nature was split into two sides like the Iroquois and the English colonists themselves. Forgotten was the time-honored unity of the League, his devout translations of the Gospels. Wholly dedicated to the British Crown and commissioned a colonel in its forces, he hurled himself into the Revolutionary War with savage ferocity.

The frightful massacre at Wyoming . . . Cherry Valley . . . the attack on Minisink . . . Oriskany . . . swift raids throughout the Mohawk Valley and on the New York–Pennsylvania border. And with every one, his reputation for bloody violence and savagery increased until he became known as "Monster Brant" to every settler on the frontier.

But like Pontiac, he had chosen the losing side. American troops moved in, laying waste to Iroquois villages, farms, orchards, and fields. The climax came when General George Washington dispatched an army of four thousand men to defeat the troops of English Tories and Brant's Iroquois in the Battle of Johnstown, ending war along the Mohawk Valley.

So fell the lofty pine, symbol of the Confederation of the Five Nations. The remaining Iroquois bewailed the end of the League:

> Now listen, ye who established the Great League. Now it has become old. Now there is nothing but wilderness. Ye are in your graves who established it. Ye have taken it with you, and have placed it under you, and there is nothing left but a desert. There ye have taken your intellects with you. Ye have placed under your heads what ye established — The Great League.

But if the Confederation of the Five Nations had perished after two hundred years, a new confederation of thirteen colonies had taken its place — The United States of America. It, too, bore the symbol of the eagle atop the pillar of its lofty ideals of liberty and justice for all men.

Fearful "Monster Brant" remained loyal to the British Crown. At the end of the Revolutionary War he was retained on half pay and given a grant of English land six miles wide on each side of the Grand

River in Ontario, Canada. In 1786 he made a second trip to England, being introduced into the Court of St. James by a close friend of the Prince of Wales. Upon his eloquent plea to His Majesty's secretary for colonial affairs, the Iroquois who had fought with him were also given an extensive land grant in Canada that became known as the Six Nations Reserve.

The rest of his life Brant lived quietly on his estate and resumed his devout translation of the Bible into Mohawk. By a third wife he had seven children. His youngest son, John, became chief of the Mohawks; and his daughter, Elizabeth, married the grandson of Sir William Johnson.

When he died, a monument was erected over his grave bearing the inscription: "This tomb was erected to the memory of Thayendanegea or Captain Joseph Brant, principal chief and warrior of Six Nations Indians, by his fellow subjects, admirers of his fidelity and attachment to the British Crown."

Red Jacket

THE FOLLOWING IS AN ADDRESS that was delivered by the Seneca orator Red Jacket at a council of the Six Nations in the summer of 1805. It was given in answer to a Christian missionary's proposal to convert the Seneca tribe.

Red Jacket, a chief of the Wolf Clan at the time of his address, was born in 1756 at Canoga, New York. He was first named Otetiani, "He Is Prepared," but took the name Sagoyewatha, "He Causes Them to Be Awake," when he became a chief. He was more widely known, however, as Red Jacket — this from the scarlet coat the British gave him for fighting on their side during the Revolutionary War.

After the war, Red Jacket became a major figure among the Senecas, and in 1792 he was invited to Philadelphia along with forty-nine other chiefs of the Iroquois Confederation to meet with George Washington. By the time the War of 1812 broke out, Red Jacket was an ally of the Americans; and he fought beside them in several skirmishes against the British.

No matter what his allegiances were, throughout his life Red Jacket remained a strong adversary of Anglo encroachment into Indian life and land. After 1815, using his considerable political and oratorical skills, he persistently called for whites to be driven out of Indian land; and in 1821 he persuaded the New York legislature to enact a law protecting reservation land.

In his last years, Red Jacket became increasingly dependent upon liquor. This and the inflexibility of his political views led to his being deposed as a chief in 1827 and losing his position on the Iroquois council. His chieftainship was later restored, partly through the effort of the United States Office of Indian Affairs, but it was not long afterward, on January 20, 1830, that the most famous orator in Seneca history died at Seneca Village, New York.

Friend and Brother: It was the will of the Great Spirit that we should meet together this day. He orders all things and has given us a fine day for our council. He has taken His garment from before the sun and caused it to shine with brightness upon us. Our eyes are opened that we see clearly; our ears are unstopped that we have been able to hear distinctly the words you have spoken. For all these favors we thank the Great Spirit, and Him only.

Brother, this council fire was kindled by you. It was at your request that we came together at this time. We have listened with attention to what you have said. You requested us to speak our minds freely. This gives us great joy; for we now consider that we stand upright before you and can speak what we think. All have heard your voice and all speak to you now as one man. Our minds are agreed. . . .

Brother, listen to what we say. There was a time when our forefathers owned this great island. Their seats extended from the rising to the setting sun. The Great Spirit had made it for the use of Indians. He had created the buffalo, the deer, and other animals for food. He had made the bear and the beaver. Their skins served us for clothing. He had caused the earth to produce corn for bread. All this He had done for His red children because He loved them. If we had some disputes about our hunting ground, they were generally settled without the shedding of much blood.

But an evil day came upon us. Your forefathers crossed the great water and landed on this island. Their numbers were small. They found friends and not enemies. They told us they had fled from their own country for fear of wicked men and had come here to enjoy their religion. They asked for a small seat. We took pity on them, granted their request, and they sat down among us. We gave them corn and meat; they gave us poison in return. . . .

They wanted more land; they wanted our country. Our eyes were opened and our minds became uneasy. Wars took place. Indians were hired to fight against Indians, and many of our people were destroyed. They also brought strong liquor among us. It was strong and powerful, and has slain thousands. . . . You have got our country, but are not satisfied; you want to force your religion upon us.

Brother, continue to listen. You say that . . . if we do not take hold of the religion which you white people teach we shall be unhappy hereafter. How do we know this to be true? We understand that your religion is written in a Book. If it was intended for us, as well as for you, why had not the Great Spirit given . . . to our forefathers the knowledge of the Book, with the means of understanding it rightly? We know only what you tell us about it. How shall we know when to believe, being so often deceived by the white people?

Brother, you say there is but one way to worship and serve the Great Spirit. If there is but one religion, why do you white people differ so much about it? Why not all agree, as you can all read the Book?

Brother. . . . We are told your religion was given to your forefathers and has been handed down from father to son. We also have a religion which was given to our forefathers and has been handed down to us, their children. We worship in that way. It teaches us to be thankful for all the favors we receive, to love each other, and to be united. We never quarrel about religion.

Brother, the Great Spirit made us all, but He has made a great difference between His white and His red children. He has given us different complexions and different customs. . . . Why may we not conclude that He has given us a different religion according to our understanding? The Great Spirit knows what is best for His children; we are satisfied.

Brother, we do not wish to destroy your religion or take it from you. We only want to enjoy our own.

Brother, you say you have not come to get our land or our money, but to enlighten our minds. I will now tell you that I have been at your meetings and saw you collect money from the meeting. . . .

Brother, we are told that you have been preaching to the white people in this place. These people are our neighbors. We are acquainted with them. We will wait a little while and see what effect your preaching has upon them. If we find it does them good, makes them honest, and less disposed to cheat Indians, we will then consider again of what you have said.

Brother, you have now heard our answer to your talk, and this is all we have to say at present. As we are going to part, we will come and take you by the hand, and hope the Great Spirit will protect you on your journey and return you safe to your friends.

Tecumseh

Tecumseh was named Shooting Star in the Shawnee tongue. And like a meteor he shot up from the dark and tragic earth to explode with a fiery flash in the heavens, leaving no trace save the brilliant flare of his passing. He was undoubtedly the greatest Indian leader, statesman, and orator in the history of his country. His avowed enemy William Henry Harrison, brigadier general, territorial governor, and ninth president of the United States, wrote of him: "He is one of those uncommon geniuses which spring up occasionally to produce revolutions and overturn the established order of things." Harrison was afraid, in fact, that Tecumseh might succeed in setting up a great Indian empire within the United States. And this was exactly what Tecumseh attempted.

He was born about 1768 in the major Shawnee town of Chillicotte on the Little Miami River, three miles north of the present Xenia, Ohio. The townsite is now farmland, and here the Shawnee tribe has erected a stone monument to mark Tecumseh's birthplace.

When Tecumseh was a boy of six, his father, a Shawnee chief, was killed while fighting American settlers pouring into the great valley of the Ohio. Tecumseh was taken care of by an older brother until he, too, died fighting for his land. Then a second brother was killed beside Tecumseh when they were fighting the incoming Americans under the Miami chief Little Turtle.

His third brother was not a warrior but a seer who was said to have had a vision of the spirit world. Shawnees called him Tenskwatawa, The Prophet. One of his dire prophecies he made in a stirring speech:

> Hear me, O deluded people, for the last time! This wide region

was once your inheritance; but now the cry of the revelry of war
is no more heard on the shores of the majestic Hudson, or on the
sweet banks of the silver Mohawk.

The eastern tribes have long since disappeared — even the
forests that sheltered them are laid low; and scarcely a trace of our
nation remains, except here and there the Indian name of a stream
or a village. And such, sooner or later, will be the fate of other
tribes; in a little while they will go the way that their brethren have
gone.

They will vanish like a vapor from the face of the earth; their
very history will be lost in forgetfulness; and the places that now
know them will know them no more. We are driven back until we
can retreat no farther; our hatchets are broken; our bows are
snapped; our fires are extinguished. A little longer and the white
man will cease to persecute us, for we shall cease to exist.

Tecumseh did not hate white men as did many of his Shawnee
warriors. He gave strict orders to his warriors: "You must not torture
any white men you take prisoners. Are we savages who have no more
control over ourselves than wild animals? No! We are a nation of
proud men fighting for the land of our forefathers. Let us fight like
men, then. Let us kill these Americans coming to kill us and take our
land. But I say to you: do not torture your prisoners!" He himself
protected many white families who appealed to him for safety.

Tecumseh had an intelligence and spirit that rose above all personal feelings — and this was what made him great. He had the vision
to see the great crisis of his people with a national perspective.

The policy of President Jefferson was to expand the swiftly growing United States by exterminating Indian tribes, then to claim the
territory of every extinct tribe according to the doctrine of paramount
sovereignty. He had tacitly ordered all Indian agents to lure tribal
"treaty chiefs" into debt in order to oblige them to sell lands which
did not actually belong to them but to their tribes. He had written,
"To promote the disposition to exchange lands which they have to

spare and which we want — we shall be glad to see the good and influential Indians among them in debt; because we observe that when these debts get beyond what the Indians can pay, they become willing to lop them off by a cession of lands."

Tecumseh knew that William Henry Harrison, appointed governor of the new Territory of Indiana in 1800, fully subscribed to the president's policy. Soon after taking office, Harrison estimated that there were only six hundred Indian warriors left in the whole valley of the Wabash, but that they were drinking up six thousand gallons of whiskey a year even though its sale was unlawful. Taking quick advantage of these "most depraved wretches on earth," he induced debt-ridden, whiskey-soaked "treaty chiefs" of five tribes to sign agreements in 1804 giving up their lands as far as the Wabash River.

Tecumseh was shocked. These "whiskey treaties" violated the great Treaty of Greenville, made in Ohio in 1795, by which the United States had guaranteed the tribes, as one people, all Ohio Valley land which had not specifically been ceded to the whites.

So on the Wabash River, near the mouth of Tippecanoe Creek, he and his brother Tenskwatawa now established a model village to unite many tribes against further encroachment. They kept coming: Shawnees, Wyandots, Ottawas, Kickapoos, and Ojibwas fleeing westward after Pontiac's defeat, and Delawares moving for the fourth time. Whiskey was forbidden. No American clothes and trade goods were sold. No Indian woman was ever to marry a white man. The people were to observe only their own customs and rituals.

The white Americans also kept coming. Indiana was now offering a bounty of fifty dollars for every Indian scalp, and many Indians were being shot by ruthless bounty hunters.

Having established a base for an alliance of tribes, Tecumseh began its formation. What he had in mind far exceeded in scope the federation of many villages and tribes within the same locality, like Pontiac's union of tribes in the Great Lakes region, the Powhatan Confederacy, or even the powerful League of the Iroquois. His was the supreme dream of a mighty Indian empire, a pan-Indian confederacy of all the western and southern tribes, to block forever the expansion of the white man's United States beyond the Ohio River.

Leaving his brother Tenskwatawa in charge of the village, he began his travels, north to the upper Missouri, east along the Ohio, south down the Mississippi. To the council of every tribe Tecumseh delivered his impassioned plea:

> Let us unite as brothers, as sons of our one Mother Earth. The land of our forefathers is still our land. We will keep all that is left us. The Ohio shall be our border. Beyond that, the white men shall not pass.

This was his simple message, his plea that kept rising to crest on the swells of his long and thunderous orations. A magnificent figure in fringed buckskins, he stood calm and firm before the gatherings. He stood not as a white man stands: chest out, belly in, shoulders drawn up, like one whose center of gravity lies in the head and the intellect. But as an Indian stands: legs slightly apart and feet rooted to the earth, shoulders and arms loose-hung, and belly slightly out and relaxed — like one whose center of gravity lies in the lower region that links him to the earth and all nature. His listeners could feel his power coming up from the earth, flowing through his body, and resounding with his deep voice over the multitude.

"Sell our land!" he thundered. "Why not sell the air, the clouds, and the great sea? Did not the Great Spirit make them all for the use of his children?"

As Tecumseh's fame spread, news of his efforts reached Harrison. To counteract him, the governor quietly made new agreements with eleven separate tribes in 1809, by which they gave up a total of three million acres extending a hundred miles up both banks of the Wabash.

It was now inevitable that Harrison and Tecumseh meet. Each recognized in the other a leader to be reckoned with, and a deadly enemy. The territorial capital of Vincennes was only 150 miles south of the village on the Tippecanoe, and Tecumseh made several trips there to protest these sales of Indian lands.

Patiently the Shawnee chief explained that to all Indians the land was a living thing, their Mother: "The Great Spirit made the earth and all that it nourishes, plant, bird and beast, for the common good of all mankind. Not for the benefit of the few, but for all. Whatever lives on the land, whatsoever grows out of the earth, and all that is in the rivers and waters flowing through it, is given jointly to all, and everyone is entitled to his share. Land cannot be sold."

It was the same view that had been presented to whites since the arrival of the English nearly two hundred years before. Harrison refused to accept it. He had been made a special commissioner to treat with Indians "on the subject of boundary or lands" for the express purpose of expanding the paramount sovereignty of the nation.

But there was a legal point involved also. "The land treaties you made in 1804 and these you have just made are invalid," asserted Tecumseh. "The United States Government does not have the right to purchase land from a single tribe. By the Treaty of Greenville it agreed to the principle of accepting cessions of land not from separate tribes, but from all of them acting in common."

"I know that treaty even though it is written on a parchment seven feet long and three feet wide, and I tell you I have bought land from eleven tribes!" answered Harrison, determined to undermine the provisions of the treaty protecting Indian interests.

"From tribes acting separately, not in common," persisted Tecumseh. "And not including the Shawnees who were not involved with the deals, and who still claim the right of occupancy."

"The right of occupancy! What is that, when we have bought the land!" exclaimed Harrison angrily.

This traditional Indian "right of occupancy" Tecumseh explained in a formal address to Governor Harrison in council at Vincennes on August 12, 1810.

ADDRESS OF TECUMSEH TO
GOVERNOR HARRISON

Delivered in council at Vincennes, Indiana,
on August 12, 1810.

It is true that I am a Shawnee. My forefathers were warriors. Their son is a warrior. From them I take only my existence; from my tribe I take nothing. I am the maker of my own fortune; and Oh! that I could make that of my red people, and of my country, as great as the conceptions of my mind, when I think of the Spirit that rules the universe. I would not then come to Governor Harrison to ask him to tear the treaty and to obliterate the landmark; but I would say to him, "Sir, you have the liberty to return to your own country."

The Being Within, communing with past ages, tells me that once, nor until lately, there was no white man on this continent; that it then all belonged to red men, children of the same parents, placed on it by the Great Spirit that made them, to keep it, to traverse it, to enjoy its productions, and to fill it with the same race, once a happy race, since made miserable by the white people who are never contented but always encroaching. The way, and the only way, to check and to stop this evil, is for all the red men to unite in claiming a common and equal right in the land, as it was at first, and should be yet; for it never was divided, but belongs to all for the use of each. For no part has a right to sell, even to each other, much less to strangers — those who want all, and will not do with less.

The white people have no right to take the land from the Indians, because they had it first; it is theirs. They may sell, but all must join. Any sale not made by all is not valid. The late sale is bad. It was made by a part only. Part do not know how to sell. It requires all to make a bargain for all. All red men have equal rights to the unoccupied land. The right of occupancy is as good *in one place as another*. There cannot be two occupations in the same place. The first excludes all others. It is not so in hunting or traveling; for there the same ground will serve many, as they may follow each other all day; but the camp is stationary, and that is occupancy. It belongs to the first who sits down on his blanket or skins which he has thrown on the ground; and till he leaves it, no other has a right.

*   *   *

"The only way to stop this evil," Tecumseh concluded, "is for all the red men to unite in claiming a common and equal right in our land. Until that is accomplished, I will not rest."

Gathering his blanket about him, he walked out of the council with his seventy-five warriors.

Tecumseh now traveled farther south in an attempt to persuade Creeks, Choctaws, and Chickasaws to join his great alliance. Governor Harrison, meanwhile, was having trouble of his own. He had lost his popularity since Madison had been elected president. The people of the territory were clamoring for the rich lands along the Wabash which he had secured from the Indians by treaty, but which were still being held by Tecumseh under "right of occupancy." A military exploit was needed to restore Harrison to favor, as he freely admitted, even at the risk of war.

Finally, when Tecumseh was down in Florida, the opportunity came for which the governor had been waiting. At the key village on the Tippecanoe, the Indians and neighboring white settlers became involved in a minor fracas. Harrison immediately led a force of nine hundred troops to the village.

Tenskwatawa, The Prophet, who was no warrior, lost his head. Instead of playing for time with parleys until Tecumseh returned, he ordered a hasty attack. The Battle of Tippecanoe, small as it was, achieved Harrison's aims. He had broken up the village, established his military reputation, and regained his popularity to the extent that he was elected president a few years later along with John Tyler as vice-president, under the slogan "Tippecanoe and Tyler, too."

Tecumseh returned to find his people scattered and disillusioned, for they believed The Prophet's word that the white men's bullets would be made harmless. This was the end of Tecumseh's grand alliance, his hope and dream.

A few months later war broke out between the British and the Americans — the War of 1812. Harrison, whose term as governor was up, was immediately commissioned brigadier general in the United States Army.

Tecumseh, undaunted, led his warriors to Canada and enlisted in the British forces. He was given command of two thousand warriors of the allied tribes, which he led into four major battles against American forces: at Frenchtown, the Raisin, Fort Meigs, and Fort Stephenson. It was no use. Like Pontiac, he had chosen the losing side.

The decisive battle on Lake Erie was won by the Americans, the British withdrawing under Major General Henry A. Proctor. Tecumseh and his Indian command covered Proctor's retreat. The British army kept retreating, Tecumseh always behind it for protection against the advancing Americans. Finally, at the Thames River in Ontario, Tecumseh ordered a halt. Here, he insisted, Proctor must make his stand. The two armies were now close together in battle formation, the American army being under command of Tecumseh's old enemy, now Major General Harrison.

That afternoon in a council meeting of British officers and Indian chiefs, Tecumseh delivered "in the name of the Indian chiefs and warriors to Major General Proctor, as representative of their Great Father, the King," his last speech:

> Father, listen to your children! You have them now all before you.
> . . . Listen! When war was declared, our Father stood and gave us
> the tomahawk, and told us that he was ready to strike the Americans;
> that he wanted our assistance, and that we would certainly get us
> our lands back, which the Americans had taken from us. . . .
> You always told us to remain here and take care of our own. It

made our hearts glad to hear that was your wish. Our Father, the King, is the head, and you represent him. You have told us you would never draw your foot off British ground; but Father, we see you are drawing back. . . . We must compare our Father's conduct to a fat animal that carries its tail upon its back, but when affrighted drops it between its legs and runs off. . . .

Father! You have got the arms and ammunition which our Great Father sent for his red children. If you have an idea of going away, give them to us, and you may go and welcome; for us our lives are in the hands of the Great Spirit. We are determined to defend our lands, and if it is His will we wish to leave our bones upon them.

That night the two opposing forces prepared for battle. Tecumseh in his tent was dressed in his customary shirt, leggings, and moccasins of buckskin, and wore a large silver brooch. Thinking of his father and two brothers who had died for their Motherland, he sat patiently waiting for the dawn. He was forty-five years old.

Who knew just what happened to him the next day? British, American, and Indian troops alike only knew that Tecumseh was at the head of his warriors when the battle began — a complete victory for General Harrison. It was said that Tecumseh's warriors carried off and hid his body so it would not be mutilated by the enemy. Others said he had not been killed at all; that he was still alive, wandering about to encourage his people to fight on for their land. Still others believed he had been miraculously spirited away by that one Great Spirit of all life to which he had given such wondrous voice.

So do all shooting stars vanish without trace.

Black Hawk

THIS IS THE STORY of a hawk whose wings were clipped by intrigue and whose pride was broken by defeat. His name was given to a war, the Black Hawk War, which lasted scarcely three months.

Black Hawk was a handsome man, sitting that day in a council of the Sauks and Foxes on the Illinois bank of the Mississippi River. He was just over sixty, and his buckskin-dressed body was still lean and straight. His hawk-like face with its long nose, luminous dark eyes, and firm mouth, gave him the commanding look of a chief. All the hair above his high forehead had been shaved off except his scalp lock, and by this one knew he was a warrior. He sat quietly listening to the speaker opposite him, but the councilmen around him knew that Black Hawk was waiting to swoop in and tear all arguments to shreds.

Since the age of fifteen, when he had scalped his first man, Black Hawk had proved himself a fighter. The council members remembered his raids against enemy tribes, and his coming back with scalps. During one raid his father had been killed. Black Hawk for five years after that had refrained from war, praying for guidance as a member of the Thunder Clan of the Sauk tribe and the son of a chief. Then he had led a war party, destroying an Osage camp of forty lodges and personally killing nine enemy warriors. On another raid against the Cherokees, he found only four men and a woman remaining in the camp. The woman he brought back captive, but the men he released because he thought it no honor to kill so few. Later he had fought with the British against the Americans in the War of 1812. It was little wonder that the councilmen looked more often at him than at the speaker, still talking after more than an hour.

"Times are changing and we must change with them," Keokuk was saying. "By the terms of the treaty we signed at St. Louis in 1804, we agreed to surrender to the government all our lands east of the Mississippi when the white settlers reached our country. Now they have come. So I say we must move west across the Mississippi as we agreed, and thus avoid war."

Keokuk, a pudgy man with coarse features, was several years younger than Black Hawk. A Sauk of the Fox Clan, he always had been sly as a fox. Black Hawk, watching him carefully, could not quite understand how he had pushed himself into the council. But Keokuk, not a chief by birth, had talked himself into power by his intrigues. As the tribal guest-keeper, he entertained visitors in his lodge, played factions of the Sauks and Foxes against each other, and cultivated the friendship of the incoming white Americans in the hope they would consider him the chief.

"We are honorable men," concluded Keokuk. "Is there not one here who himself confirmed the treaty in 1816?"

Black Hawk rose. "What is this talk of honor? I touched the goose quill to that treaty, it is true — not knowing that by that act I consented to give away my own village of Saukenuk, our Rock River homeland, all our tribal lands in Illinois and Wisconsin. Had that been explained to me, I should have opposed it.

"What do we know of the manner of laws and customs of the white people? They might buy our bodies for dissection and we would touch the goose quill to confirm it, without knowing what we were doing."

"You signed it!" accused Keokuk.

Black Hawk continued, "My reason teaches me that land cannot be sold. The Great Spirit gave it to his children to live upon. So long as they occupy and cultivate it, they have a right to the soil. Nothing can be sold but such things as can be carried away. The Sauks and Foxes will remain on their land."

"They will not!" shouted Keokuk, jumping to his feet. "They will move across the Great River with me!"

So it began that day in council — the quarrel between Black Hawk and Keokuk which split the Sauk and Fox tribes into opposing groups. In 1820, Keokuk, friendly to the white people, moved his supporters across the Mississippi into Iowa. Black Hawk, with his supporters, remained in his home village of Saukenuk. It was situated on the Rock River just above its confluence with the Mississippi, where Rock Island, Illinois, now stands. The soil produced rich crops; from the river his people obtained all the fish they needed; and the English trader there, George Davenport, was most friendly.

"You'd better move across the Mississippi into Iowa with Keokuk," he advised Black Hawk.

Black Hawk was worried. He paddled up Rock River to seek advice from two friends. One of them was White Cloud, whom some people called a prophet. He was half Winnebago and half Sauk, six feet tall, fat, and gloomy. He smoked a pipe with a stem two feet long, and unlike most Indians wore a black mustache. The other one was Neapope, nicknamed "The Broth," considered wily, shrewd, and deceitful. Both of them advised Black Hawk that the Potawatomis and Winnebagos would help him defend his homeland.

"What is a man to do when he gets different advice from his friends?" wondered Black Hawk.

It was decided for him when he found that the trader Davenport had bought the site of Saukenuk. Davenport now owned the very piece of ground on which stood Black Hawk's own lodge, as well as his people's graveyard! More settlers came, taking farmland around the village. To add to Black Hawk's worries, a band of Menominees was marching down from the north to revenge the deaths of some of their people at the hands of Sauk and Fox warriors. Then Black Hawk heard that Governor John Reynolds of Illinois had ordered the militia to march upon his village.

Black Hawk retreated across the Mississippi with his people, leaving the advancing soldiers to burn all the lodges of Saukenuk. But he rallied his people with stinging words: "Look at yourselves now! A homeless people! Will you stay here as exiles with Keokuk's band? Will you give up your homeland without a struggle? The Winnebagos and Potawatomis will help us win back our land!"

Gaining the support of some two thousand men, women, and children, he recrossed the Mississippi early in April 1832 and started up Rock River. Here he learned Neapope had lied to him; only a small band of Winnebagos was waiting to join him. Continuing up Rock River into Wisconsin, Black Hawk and his homeless warriors roamed through the Lake Koshkonong swamp country and attacked frontier settlements.

In the meantime, Governor Reynolds, aroused by public outcry, hastily recruited a large force of mounted volunteers for the state militia. Elected captain of one of the companies was a lanky clerk from Denton Offutt's store in New Salem named Abraham Lincoln. After marching north for a month, the grumbling volunteers took a vote whether to continue to chase Black Hawk or to leave the field. The vote was a tie. Whereupon Governor Reynolds discharged them and called for new volunteers. Lincoln reenlisted and was marched north to Fort Deposit, where the volunteers joined regular army troops under the command of General Henry Atkinson, whom Black Hawk knew as "White Beaver."

General Atkinson, taking charge of the campaign against Black Hawk, sent General James D. Henry with one force and General Henry Dodge with another, to cover the west side of the swamp. He himself with a detachment of regulars, and General Milton K. Alexander with a brigade of volunteers, moved up the east side. Lincoln was not included. He was mustered out when he reached the Lake Koshkonong country and saw no fighting.

Meanwhile, Black Hawk and his refugees were having a miserable time. In the marshy country they were forced to dig roots for food. And now, with regular army troops and state militia led by generals galore menacing him on all sides, he fled west, intending to descend the Wisconsin River to the Mississippi.

When he reached the river on an afternoon in late July, the troops of Henry and Dodge caught up with him. The only means of escape was to cross to the west side of the river where bluffs rose called the Wisconsin Heights. The women tore bark from the trees in order to float their babies and children across to an island while Sauk and Fox warriors fought off the troops. What the Indian casualties were no one knew. Estimates ranged from forty to one hundred Indians killed to one white.

At nightfall the troops withdrew, and Black Hawk continued his flight west across southern Wisconsin. For ten days his band plodded on, half-starved, their clothes in rags, most of them without moccasins. Black Hawk urged them on without rest: "On the far side of the Mississippi we will be safe."

Finally they reached the Mississippi near the mouth of the little Black Ax River. As they were cutting trees to serve as canoes and rafts, disaster struck again. Even as Black Hawk looked, there sounded a shrill whistle, and the steamship *Warrior* puffed into view. "Give me a white flag!" shouted Black Hawk. "I will go aboard for a talk!"

Just as he began to wave it, the captain of the steamer opened fire with a field piece, killing twenty-five Indians. There was no crossing the Mississippi now under the deadly fire that swept the bank till dark. All that night the fireless encampment echoed with the wails of women and frightened children. "At dawn we will escape to the north!" Black Hawk kept pleading. "There we will be safe!"

But that morning General Atkinson's pursuing force of thirteen hundred regulars and volunteers caught up with them. Squeezed between the troops and the river, the Indians had no means of escape. Everywhere Black Hawk looked, he saw old men, women, and children being shot down or driven into the river to drown. In despair he hoisted a flag of truce. It was ignored. The Battle of Black Ax went on. General Winfield Scott later apologized for the frightful toll of women and children; in the brush, he said, his troops could not distinguish them from the Indian warriors.

Black Hawk, Neapope, and other refugees fled north. Black Hawk reached a Winnebago village. Here the Winnebagos betrayed him to the whites for a bribe of twenty horses and one hundred dollars, and the promise of a word about their good conduct to the Great Father in Washington. He was taken to Prairie du Chien, Wisconsin, to surrender to General J. M. Street. Black Hawk's flight was over. Yet like a captured bird, he was still proud and defiant as he made his speech of surrender.

BLACK HAWK'S SPEECH OF SURRENDER

Delivered on August 27, 1832,
at Prairie du Chien, Wisconsin, when
he surrendered to General J. M. Street.

You have taken me prisoner with my warriors. I am much grieved; for I expected, if I did not defeat you, to hold out much longer and give you more trouble before I surrendered. . . .

Black Hawk is now a prisoner of the white men; they will do with him as they wish. But he can stand torture, and is not afraid of death. He is no coward.

Black Hawk is an Indian. He has done nothing for which an Indian ought to be ashamed. He has fought for his countrymen against white men who came, year after year, to cheat them and take away their lands.

You know the cause of our making war. It is known to all white men. The white men despise the Indians, and drive them from their homes. They smile in the face of the poor Indian, to cheat him; they shake him by the hand, to gain his confidence; they make him drunk, to deceive him.

We told them to let us alone, and keep away from us; but they followed on and beset our paths, and coiled themselves among us like the snake. They poisoned us by their touch. We were not safe. We lived in danger. We looked up to the Great Spirit. We went to our Father (in Washington). We were encouraged. His council gave us fair words and big promises, but we got no satisfaction; things were growing worse. There were no deer in the forest. The opossum and beaver fled. The springs were drying up, and our squaws and papooses were without food to keep them from starving. . . .

We set up the war whoop, and dug up the tomahawk; our knives were ready, and the heart of Black Hawk swelled high in his bosom when he led his warriors to battle. He is satisfied. He will go to the world of spirits contented. He has done his duty. His father will meet him there and command him. . . .

Farewell, my nation! . . . He can do no more. He is near his end. His sun is setting, and will rise no more.

Farewell to Black Hawk!

He was then handed over in chains to a young lieutenant, Jefferson Davis, who was later to become president of the Southern Confederacy. Davis conducted him to Jefferson Barracks, Missouri, from where Black Hawk was transferred to Fortress Monroe, Virginia. After ten months' confinement, he was taken on tour through several eastern cities, given presents by officials, and presented to President Andrew Jackson in the White House.

The indomitable old chief was still not tamed. He greeted the president brusquely: "I am a man and you are another!" During their brief conversation he said, "I took up the hatchet to revenge injuries which my people could no longer endure. Had I borne them without striking, my people would have said, 'Black Hawk is a woman; he is too old to be a chief; he is no Sauk.' "

President Jackson duly presented Black Hawk with a military uniform and a sword, but soon afterward ordered that Keokuk instead of Black Hawk be made chief of the Sauks and Foxes. The two rivals were together when army officers announced news of the appointment. Black Hawk, with anger and contempt, whipped off his breechclout and slapped Keokuk across the face with it.

"I am a man!" he cried. "I will not obey the counsels of anyone! I will act for myself. No one shall govern me!"

Eventually, however, his pride broken at last, the aging warrior was forced by necessity to settle on the Des Moines River near Iowaville, on the reservation governed by Keokuk. Sitting in front of his lodge, listening to the news brought him by red and white friends alike, he knew that his own defeat had marked the end of independence for all prairie tribes east of the Great River. The Kickapoos had ceded Illinois. The Ojibwas and Ottawas had given up Michigan, and the Miamis their last land in Indiana. Oshkosh, named a Menominee chief by United States commissioners, had signed a treaty surrendering his tribe's land in Wisconsin. The Potawatomi tribe had been deported to the land west. From the Atlantic to the Mississippi, the great white wave had swamped tribe after tribe.

Finally accepting their inevitable defeat without bitterness, Black Hawk assented to make a speech at a Fourth of July celebration near Fort Madison:

> Brothers! It has pleased the Great Spirit that I am here today. I have eaten with my white friends. The earth is our mother; we are on it, with the Great Spirit above us. It is good. I hope we are all friends here.
>
> A few winters ago I was fighting against you. I did wrong perhaps; but that is past; it is buried; let it be forgotten.
>
> Rock River was a beautiful country. I liked my towns, my cornfields, and the home of my people. I fought for it. It is now yours; keep it as we did; it will produce you good crops.
>
> I thank the Great Spirit that I am now friendly with my white brothers. We are here together; we have eaten together; we are friends. It is His wish and mine.
>
> I was once a great warrior. I am now poor. Keokuk has been the cause of my present condition; but do not attach blame to him.
>
> I am now old. I have looked upon the Mississippi since I have been a child. I love the Great River. I have dwelt upon its banks from

the time I was an infant. I look upon it now. I shake hands with
you, and as it is my wish, I hope you are my friends.

When Black Hawk died shortly afterward, in 1838, his body was
seated on the prairie underneath a shelter, according to custom. It was
dressed in his military uniform, decorated with medals from President
Jackson, John Quincy Adams, and the city of Boston; and a cane from
Henry Clay was placed between his knees — gifts from those enemies
he had fought so courageously and had finally accepted as his friends,
brothers, and sons of his own Mother Earth.

Cherokee Alphabet.

Sequoyah

He had a way with words, this tall handsome man so admired by young women even though he had a wife. You could tell this by the way he held his neighbors spellbound with his stories, especially after he'd had some drinks from a bottle. And he entertained them often instead of plowing his cornfield, planting potatoes, or chopping wood. There was nothing else about Sequoyah to suggest that he would illuminate one of the brightest pages in the history of his tribe. But he had genius, and genius has a way of overcoming all handicaps.

No one knew just who his father was. Perhaps he was a German peddler named George Guest, who had strayed into the wild mountain fastnesses of Tennessee shortly before the Revolutionary War. Others claimed he was Nathaniel Gist, a friend of George Washington, who came to enlist Cherokees to fight for the colonies against England. Whoever he was, he married a Cherokee woman in the village of Tuskegee on the Tennessee River, a few miles from the Cherokee capital of Echota. Soon after she gave birth to Sequoyah, her husband wandered off, leaving his son to grow up as a Cherokee.

Although Sequoyah was often called George Gist or Guest, he preferred his Cherokee name and was always proud of his Indian heritage. The Cherokee Nation, one of the Five Civilized Tribes of the South, spread over southern Tennessee and the Carolinas, and northern Alabama and Georgia. To the south, the powerful Creeks occupied central Georgia and Alabama; the Chickasaws and Choctaws, Mississippi; and the Seminoles, Florida.

Life was simple. The Cherokees lived in one-room cabins with dirt floors, raised corn, potatoes, and a few head of livestock, and hunted game in the mountains. But what beautiful country it was! The hills blossomed with azaleas, mountain laurel, rhododendrons, and star magnolias; and over all this, the Great Smokies cast their bluish haze.

There were no schools in the remote settlements, and Sequoyah had not learned to speak or write English when a friend brought him a few printed pages stolen from a captured white man. "Look!" He pointed out to Sequoyah the marks on the paper. "They are a spell cast on the paper so it will talk to other white men far off and even on another day. Talking leaves!"

Sequoyah puzzled over the marks a long time. "No, they are not magic at all. Some white men invented these marks just like others invented the pieces of metal that make their guns shoot. See here." With his knife he traced a mark on a flat stone. "I myself could invent such writing marks for us Cherokees."

"Why don't you do it then?" laughed his friend.

Sequoyah was too busy doing nothing, but he remembered the idea.

He began to prepare for his task, in a roundabout way, during the War of 1812. Becoming known as Red Sticks, the Creeks declared war against the Americans by their usual custom of erecting a red pole in the center of their village. Fiery General Andrew Jackson set out on a Creek campaign, enlisting friendly Cherokees in his command. Sequoyah was one of them.

After the Battle of Horseshoe Bend in Alabama, which ended the campaign, Sequoyah limped home. Whether he had been injured in the battle or a hunting accident no one knew, but he had a lame leg for life. He was also disillusioned. For the American government, having defeated both the English and the Creeks, was extending its national boundaries by appropriating Indian land. The territories of Georgia and Alabama were established on land taken from the Creeks and Cherokees, and Mississippi from Choctaw and Chickasaw country. Many of the dispossessed Indians fled to Florida. About half of the Cherokees concentrated in northern Georgia, establishing their capital at New Echota.

Here Sequoyah married a Cherokee girl with the English name of Sally, the first of his successive five wives. New Echota was a backwoods settlement of a few log cabins where the chiefs met in council and held court. Sequoyah took no interest in these events. No longer was he a jolly storyteller and drinking companion, nor could he participate in the ancient Cherokee game of stickball. Leaving his wife to do the farm work, he shut himself up alone in a cabin day after day, month upon month.

"How queer! What is he doing in there?" neighbors demanded of his wife.

"How should I know?" she snapped back. "Don't you see me plowing behind this stubborn mule all day?"

Sequoyah in his cabin, spectacles on his nose, a foot-long pipe between his teeth, kept carving little marks on a slab of bark with his knife.

Sometimes he straddled the old mule and rode north to Spring Place, where the Moravian Brethren had established the first missionary school among the Cherokees. In the classroom he would squat down on a bench with the children, pouring over their simple textbooks.

"So you want to learn to read and write English," the missionary teacher observed. "That's what the Cherokees need."

"It's not enough. White men's writing is good only for white men. We Cherokee must learn to write our own language."

The teacher smiled kindly and gave him a speller to take home. "This will be better. Cherokee is a difficult language to speak. No one will ever be able to write it."

Back home, Sequoyah continued his work. Like the ancient Chinese and Egyptians, he was inventing a character for each Cherokee word. Each was a tiny picture he painted on paper with a fine brush.

Sequoyah enjoyed this, for he was a good artist with imagination. Soon Turtle Fields came to call.

"I must warn you, Sequoyah, that people are becoming worried. You have either gone mad or you're making a fool of yourself."

"Maybe, but what I'm doing won't make fun of the Cherokees." He adjusted the spectacles on his nose, took a puff of sumac from his long pipe, and showed Turtle Fields some of the marks he had made. "A word is like a wild animal. White men have learned to catch these animals and put them to work on paper. That is why they are wise and powerful. We Cherokee are wise, too, but our wisdom dies with us. Our words are forgotten. So I am inventing for Cherokees a writing that will preserve our language and our wisdom long after our speakers are dead."

He continued work on his "talking leaves," but he was growing discouraged. The more characters he invented, the more words there were to use. Everything had a name! Why, there were as many words as there were leaves in the forest! And if he himself forgot his characters as fast as he invented them, how could he expect others to remember them?

Dedicated scholar that he was, Sequoyah labored steadily for some four years. But his neighbors became increasingly more alarmed, for none of them could understand what he was up to. "Talking leaves" indeed! Could he be one of those making spells to bring evil upon them? The suspicion that witchcraft was being worked grew stronger when a cow died in calving, and an untimely hailstorm cut down all their young corn. Organizing a witch-hunt, the Cherokees put to death a family suspected of witchcraft, sparing only one woman member because she was pregnant. Misfortunes continued. And now neighbors gathered to name Sequoyah as the guilty one.

"Shall it be death?" the leader asked.

"He is quiet and gives us no other trouble," one man spoke in a doubting voice.

"He's making spells!" insisted another.

"Perhaps he is just a little mad, having lost his reason over those 'talking leaves' of his," answered a friend of Sequoyah.

"And what do you say?" the leader asked Sequoyah's wife.

"It is true he neglects his family, leaving me to do a man's work in the fields!" she answered crossly. "Still, I cannot say my own husband is guilty of witchcraft. Maybe if we stopped him from his crazy doings all would be well."

"But how?"

"I have a plan," she answered. "Listen."

The next day she induced Sequoyah to leave his cabin on the pretext that he was needed to look at a sick cow. As soon as he was out of sight, she signaled the waiting neighbors. The enraged neighbors rushed into the clearing and burned down the cabin with all of Sequoyah's years of work.

Sequoyah came back to watch the smoking ruins with a calm face. "Well, I was doing it the wrong way. Now I must do it again in a different manner."

His life had been spared, but the neighborhood was no longer a safe place to work. Leaving his family, he went to Washington with Chief Jolly and a group of fourteen Cherokees. The head chief, Pathkiller, spoke no English and was getting too old to serve as a spokesperson for his people. So Chief Jolly had taken upon himself the task of improving relations between the Cherokee Nation and the American government.

In Washington Sequoyah learned that the government was pressing the Cherokees for still more land, offering to exchange for it some land in Arkansas. Chief Jolly and his group, without consulting their own national council, agreed to the exchange. Maybe Sequoyah was still thinking of the new work he must do. So he, too, foolishly signed the treaty and left for Arkansas with some three hundred Cherokee emigrants anxious to avoid war with the American government.

The Cherokee council, enraged at the betrayal, passed a law

pronouncing the death penalty on any Cherokee who thereafter made any such unlawful land agreements. Sequoyah was unaware that he was now in disfavor with the whole Cherokee Nation as well as with his own neighbors back home. He was too busy in Arkansas trying to devise a new system for writing the Cherokee language. He had found after years of patient work that the invention of a character for every word wouldn't do. What should he try next?

Now for another three years he experimented. Then suddenly in 1821 the idea came to him in a flash of inspiration. Find all the syllables spoken in the Cherokee tongue and invent a character for each! Within a month it was done. There on a single piece of paper before him was a Cherokee syllabary, or alphabet, of eighty-six characters. Some of them looked like English letters, others like Greek, Egyptian, or Chinese characters, and still others were ones he had invented himself. But the system worked. All one had to do was to know the sounds they represented, and he could write the Cherokee language without bothering about spelling.

To prove it, Sequoyah transcribed a message from the Arkansas Cherokee to their people in the Nation and carried it back to New Echota. He was not warmly received. The council listened to him read the message but could not believe it was contained in the strange marks on the paper; he had probably memorized it. In despair he recorded in Cherokee the testimony in a case being tried in court, and then had his six-year-old daughter, who had not been there, read it back to the council. The chiefs were still not impressed with his brilliant achievement in devising the first Indian writing system north of Mexico — a work of genius that had accomplished in a decade what had taken the white race centuries to evolve. Sequoyah trudged home to the family he had neglected too long, and spent a sleepless night.

Early the next morning, one of the witnesses who had been in court, Big Rattling Gourd, came to see him. He had not slept either. "What you did yesterday didn't seem remarkable in daylight. But last night it did. I lay awake thinking about it. Sequoyah, do you suppose

I could learn those writing marks?"

News of Sequoyah's alphabet spread like wildfire. It usually took Cherokee children four years in school to learn to read and write English. Now within a month they could learn to read and write Cherokee. It became a game they all began to play. Young girls and old women learned the syllabary while they were weaving in their cabins. Men memorized it while resting their horses in the cornfields. Within a year thousands of Cherokees had mastered their own language.

The chiefs on the council now awarded Sequoyah a silver medal and granted him a small annuity. More important, they voted $1,500 — one-fifth of the yearly income of the Cherokee Nation — for the purchase of a printing press and type in his alphabet. Soon they had a weekly paper, the *Cherokee Phoenix*, the first newspaper in the United States printed in an Indian language. Parts of the New Testament were translated into Cherokee, and a Cherokee speller transliterating Cherokee into English letters was published. Word was sent that no more teachers should be sent; all the Cherokee Nation needed to become completely literate was lots of paper and ink.

Sequoyah, now over sixty years old, was a famous man at last. A curious figure, he looked like an Oriental potentate as he walked down the muddy street in his loose tunic, a flowered turban on his head, the silver medal strung around his throat, and smoking his long, thin-stemmed pipe. But success did not change him. He returned to his hard life in Arkansas.

By terms of a treaty with the government, he and his Cherokee neighbors traded their land in Arkansas for a tract in nearby Indian Territory and moved up the Arkansas River to Skin Bayou. Sequoyah's new home was ten acres of cleared land about fifteen miles from Fort Smith, Arkansas. Here he settled down with his family in three log cabins. He had two mules, three yoke oxen, and a few cattle. Often the family would go to his salt lick, several miles away, to prepare salt. It was difficult work: cutting wood, boiling the salt water in huge kettles until the water evaporated, and then drying the salt to sell in town.

Meanwhile, he began working out an adaptation of his Cherokee syllabary to the Choctaw language. "By this means," he explained to his friends, "the Indians of all tribes in the United States will gradually become literate in their own languages, and develop a true Indian civilization."

His hope seemed likely to come true. The Cherokee Nation, largely through his help, had now indeed proved itself one of the great civilized tribes in America. Its citizens had learned to read and write in their own language, and had compiled a written code of laws in English. They had abandoned their simple tribal organization of clans, adopting a form of government that made it a republic like the United States. They had formulated a constitution. Always a hard-working people who loved their land, they were becoming so prosperous as farmers and stock raisers that many of them owned Negro slaves. They had proved, Sequoyah insisted, that a tribe of illiterate Indians without help from outside was capable of creating a nation as civilized as any in the world.

Riding muleback to the Dwight Mission for his weekly copies of the *Cherokee Phoenix*, Sequoyah confidently expected this tremendous achievement to be acclaimed by white men everywhere. Instead, he was appalled by tragic news the paper printed.

The state of Georgia was incensed that a tribe of Indians within its borders should call itself a nation. It had passed laws forbidding Cherokees to sell land independently on pain of death, and outlawing tribal Indian governments. All the Cherokee Nation's laws were declared null and void, and no Cherokee could testify in a court case involving a white man.

Worse news followed. Gold was discovered on Cherokee land; and thousands of white Georgians rushed in, protected by the state militia. The Cherokee Nation, instead of fighting, carried its case against Georgia to the United States Supreme Court. The famous Chief Justice John Marshall rendered the decision:

> The Cherokee Nation, then, is a distinct community, occupying

its own territory, with boundaries accurately described, in which the laws of Georgia have no right to enter, but with the assent of the Cherokees themselves, or in conformity with treaties, and with the acts of Congress.

If Sequoyah's hopes were raised by this ruling, they were destroyed when he read President Andrew Jackson's retort: "John Marshall has rendered his decision; now let him enforce it."

Instead of upholding the Supreme Court's decision, the Congress passed an Indian Removal Act providing for the removal of all Cherokees, Creeks, Chickasaws, Choctaws, and Seminoles to the west of the Mississippi. No official of the Cherokee Nation had agreed to its provisions, and sixteen thousand Cherokees signed a petition of protest. The noted orator Edward Everett also protested to Congress in a stirring speech which ended with the solemn warning:

> The subtleties which satisfy you will not satisfy the severe judgment of enlightened Europe. Our friends there will view this measure with sorrow and our enemies alone with joy. And we ourselves, Sir, when the interest and passion of the day are past, shall look back on it, I fear, with self-reproach and regret as bitter as unavailing.

Then Sequoyah stopped receiving copies of the *Cherokee Phoenix*; Georgia had suppressed it. These were anxious months for him now, as little by little more news trickled in. Georgia was awarding Cherokee homes and farms to white settlers by a state lottery. Still his people refused to leave their homeland. Then General Winfield Scott with seven thousand troops arrived to remove them.

And now it began — the forced removal of thirteen thousand Cherokees to Indian Territory over what they called Nura-da-ut-sun'y, the "Trail of Tears." Months later Sequoyah met them at Little Rock: a broken people, forty-six hundred of whom had died from disease, privation, and exposure along the way. Here the wife of the principal chief, John Ross, died. After her burial Sequoyah helped Ross to settle their people on the reservation into which the remnants of sixty-eight Indian tribes were being herded. A new Cherokee capital was established at Tahlequah, and a government was formed.

"This will not be the end of the Cherokee Nation!" he proudly asserted. "Nor will it be the end of the Cherokees' history and traditions. As long as their language exists and spreads, they will be remembered!"

He was still a scholar. And in 1842, at the age of eighty-two, he set out to search for a band of Cherokees supposed to have vanished long ago into the mountains of the Southwest, and to seek traces of their speech among other tribes.

Three years later, when he had not been heard from, a Cherokee named Oo-no-leh went in search of him. In a letter written in Cherokee he reported meeting a Cherokee named Standing Rock who said he had witnessed Sequoyah's death and burial near the village of San Fernando in the state of Tamaulipas, Mexico. This report was never confirmed. For many years various searchers have gone to Mexico without finding any trace of what happened to Sequoyah.

When the Indian Territory applied for admission as a state in the union, the Indians by majority vote approved giving the name of Sequoyah to the state. The national administration rejected this, selecting the name Oklahoma instead. Yet Sequoyah is not forgotten. His enduring monument is that long-lived tree, the giant redwood which bears his name.

MEMORIAL

From the Cherokee Nation to the Congress
of the United States, December 29, 1835.

In truth, our cause is your own. It is the cause of liberty and justice. It is based upon your own principles, which we have learned from yourselves; for we have gloried to count your Washington and your Jefferson our great teachers.... We have practiced their precepts with success. And the result is manifest. The wilderness of forest has given place to comfortable dwellings and cultivated fields. . . . Mental culture, industrial habits, and domestic enjoyments have succeeded the rudeness of the savage state. We have learned your religion also. We have read your sacred books. Hundreds of our people have embraced their doctrines, practiced the virtues they teach, cherished the hopes they awaken. . . . We speak to the representatives of a Christian country; the friends of justice; the patrons of the oppressed. And our hopes revive, and our prospects brighten, as we indulge the thought. On your sentence our fate is suspended. . . . On your kindness, on your humanity, on your compassion, on your benevolence, we rest our hopes. . . .

Osceola

KNOWN AS The Tiger of the Swamps or Swamp Fox, he had the
easy grace of an animal as he walked through great swamps where
alligators coughed hoarsely in the dark bayous and the pink flamingo
called to its mate.

His tall, spare frame was clothed in a loose tunic and knee-high
moccasins, and on his head he wore a turban from which drooped two
large feathers. Beneath it, his glossy black hair hung to his shoulders,
and around his throat were strung necklaces of beads and Spanish
silver. Yet it was his face that attracted everyone's attention. With its
large dark eyes, wide nostrils, and full lips, it was expressive of every
mood. It could change from a look of savage ferocity to gentle kindness,
and then to a brooding melancholy. This last expression appeared most
often. For Osceola was born in a tragic era, and in his short life he ex-
perienced more pain and grief than his sensitive nature could bear.

That early April morning in 1835, Osceola emerged from Wahoo
Swamp in north-central Florida and strode quickly across the savanna
to the clump of wooden buildings that comprised Fort King. The
place was crowded with Seminoles and Creeks, and in the big conference room the peace council was already in session. The meeting had
been called by the Indian agent for the Seminoles, General Wiley
Thompson, who sat at the center of the table surrounded by thirteen
Indian chiefs. Osceola slumped down along the wall with other Seminoles and listened to the talk.

It concerned the treaty made at Payne's Landing on the Oklawaha
River three years before. General Thompson, one of the sponsors of

the treaty, explained that by it the Seminoles had agreed to surrender all their lands and remove west of the Mississippi with the Creeks within three years.

The chiefs began to mutter. "It is true Charley Emathla and other chiefs signed a treaty, but without consent of the Seminole Nation."

"Why is it no Negro will be allowed to accompany us? Does not Washington know that many slaves have escaped to live with us? We have married them, have had children by them. Would you break up our families when we move to a far land?"

"The Congress of the white chiefs in Washington passed the Indian Removal Act," answered General Thompson. "It is the law that all the Five Civilized Tribes — the Creeks, Cherokees, Chickasaws, Choctaws, and you Seminoles — must remove to Indian Territory. Now your three years are almost up. So I ask you to acknowledge the treaty in order that you may get ready to leave."

He spread out on the table a paper for the chiefs to sign.

Some of them nodded surlily. Others stood up, arms folded over their breasts, saying nothing. Suddenly Osceola jumped forward, and drawing his knife plunged it through the treaty.

"This is our answer!" he cried. "The Seminole will never be taken from their land."

There was a moment of shocked silence. Osceola was not a chief, and so not expected to voice an opinion. Then Thompson called the guards. "Seize that man and put him in irons!" And Osceola was led away.

A few days later, after several friendly chiefs had interceded for him, he was released on his promise to return with his followers and acknowledge the removal agreement. In five days he came back with seventy-nine Seminoles, pretended to agree with Thompson, and was released.

Thompson was elated. "I now have no doubt of his sincerity, and as little that the greatest difficulty is surmounted." But Thompson did not know Seminoles, having been in his post only a short time; and he did not know that Osceola was a dedicated enemy of the whites and had now emerged as the greatest leader of the Seminoles.

Still a young man, Osceola had a bitter history behind him. The Creek Nation was a Muskhogean-speaking confederacy of fifty towns spread over Alabama and Georgia. The Lower Creeks, as they were called, were concentrated along the Chattahoochee River on the Alabama-Georgia border, and the Upper Creeks along the Coosa and Tallapoosa rivers. Here, on the banks of the Tallapoosa, Osceola was born in 1803. His mother was the daughter of a town chief, a *Tustenusee*, and after the death of his father, married a white man named Powell. It was said that Osceola's paternal grandfather was a Scotsman. Whatever his ancestry, Osceola grew up a Creek. When he was nine years old, the Creeks allied themselves with the British against the Americans in the War of 1812, bringing on the Creek War. They were defeated by General Andrew Jackson at the Battle of Horseshoe Bend in Alabama, only seventy of their nine hundred warriors being left alive. In retribution, the government appropriated more than half their land.

Osceola, with thousands of other Creeks and other Indians from Georgia and Alabama, fled to Florida. Here they intermarried with runaway Negro slaves and the last survivors of the original Florida tribes — Calusas, Temucuses, and Apaluchees. The amalgamation resulted in a new people whom the northern Creeks called Isty-Semole, which meant "wild man." But in 1817 General Andrew Jackson in the First Seminole War quelled their uprising and forced Spain to cede the peninsula of Florida to the United States. In this campaign Osceola, only fifteen years old, saw his first fighting.

Soon afterward he moved to the vicinity of Fort King, southwest of St. Augustine, and married Che-cho-ter, the daughter of a Seminole chief and a fugitive Negro slave. To support them, Osceola served as a scout at the fort. Here he learned what was happening to the Creeks back in Georgia.

William MacIntosh, the half-breed chief of the Lower Creeks who was in the pay of Georgia land commissioners, had ceded fifteen million acres of Creek land to Georgia, allowing $250,000 to compensate Georgia for slaves who had fled to Florida. Three years later he had signed another treaty ceding ten million more acres to Georgia. This was resented by thirty-six chiefs representing nine-tenths of the Creek Nation because it was a violation of the Creek law which provided for the death penalty to any Creek who sold land without consent of the Creek Nation. Hence a formal sentence was passed on MacIntosh, who was executed by Menewa, a former Red Stick chief.

Osceola kept this in mind should the Seminoles be betrayed by one of their chiefs. Leaving his post, he joined the Miccosukees, a band of Seminoles living near Lake Miccosukee. As a sub-chief, he observed the Seminole chiefs carefully and often talked about them to his young wife at home.

"Micanope, the head chief, is fat and lazy," he said to her.

Che-cho-ter did not reply. Their house, like the others in the compound, was a thatched shelter raised on poles above the ground. Here Osceola loved to sit and watch her as she prepared supper below. In the flare of the sinking sun, her young dark body looked like velvet. She was making *conte*, his favorite dish, pounding the roots of China briar to a pulp, mixing it with water, then straining it to dry beside the fire.

"Jumper is the most influential chief in council, but he does little more than talk," he said again.

Che-cho-ter examined the drying powder, then mixed in it a little warm water and honey, and set it aside to cool into a jelly.

"There are other chiefs, Philip, Yahaloochee, Co-e-harjo," continued Osceola, "and Charley Emathla, whom I distrust. But no leader." He swung down from the shelter and stood in front of the corn cakes cooking on the fire.

The sun had set. Che-cho-ter's dark body was absorbed by the night, but in the light of the coals the whites of her eyes shone palely. She suddenly grasped both his arms. "Osceola, I am afraid!" she said in a tremulous voice. "I smell the smell of evil. I hear the sound of war and death approaching. Be careful!"

He put his arms around her. "I hear nothing. I smell nothing. Come. Our corn cakes are cooked, our *conte* is cool."

There came the morning when he watched her leave to do her trading at Fort King. It was the last time he ever saw her. Wild with anxiety, he finally learned that she had been captured at the fort and sold into slavery. General Wiley Thompson declaimed any knowledge of this.

"How could I know anything about it? Slave traders, whiskey peddlers, all the riffraff and bobtail in the country are swarming into Florida!"

"You're the commander of this fort and the agent for the Seminoles!" stormed Osceola. "I hold you responsible for whatever happened to her. Do not forget this!"

Nor did Osceola forget it when, that April morning in 1835, he plunged his knife into Thompson's paper and asserted himself as the natural leader of the Seminoles. Almost immediately things began to happen.

The Seminoles' three-year period of grace before their removal was almost up. They were ordered to assemble at Tampa Bay to board transports to take them up the Mississippi on their way to Indian Territory. But in late November, hardly a month before the sailing date, Charley Emathla, the Seminole chief who had signed the removal treaty, was murdered. Thompson was sure that Osceola had ordered his execution.

A month later General Thompson and one of his lieutenants were walking outside the fort when Osceola and a band of Seminoles shot and killed them. Thompson's body was riddled with fourteen bullets. At least one of them was fired from the rifle he once had given Osceola in hope of winning his friendship. After scalping the two men, Osceola and his band rushed to the home of the fort's sutler, killing him and two clerks. Uttering a piercing war cry that all the garrison could identify, Osceola led his men off towards the swamp.

That same afternoon a military force under Major Francis L. Dade was marching to Fort King to enforce the removal when it was ambushed by Osceola and his men. Of its 8 officers and 102 men, all were killed except 3. Two of these died shortly afterwards from their wounds.

That night, deep in Wahoo Swamp, Osceola and his Seminole warriors celebrated with a great feast of venison, bear's ribs, hominy, and corn cakes. Osceola, sitting morosely by the fire, was given a dish of his favorite *conte*. He tasted it, threw it away. No one could ever make *conte* like Che-cho-ter. But he had killed Thompson. The thought was reassuring. The fires were leaping higher. A drum was beating. Hillis Higher Harjo, the medicine chief, was beginning the Scalp Dance. Osceola got up and walked to the pole from which hung Thompson's scalp. He spat at it, addressed it profanely, and then began to dance around it.

All Florida knew that night that the Second Seminole War had begun.

General Duncan L. Clinch, who had arrived with an army to enforce the removal of Seminoles, knew it too. He received a letter from Osceola which read briefly: "You have guns and so have we. You have powder and lead, and so have we. You have men and so have we. Your men will fight and so will ours, till the last drop of the Seminoles' blood has moistened the dust of his hunting ground."

Now a game of cat-and-mouse began in the Florida swamps. One army commander after another came to round up Osceola and his Seminoles. The Tiger of the Swamps led the commands into the swamps, attacked, and then vanished. General Edmund P. Gaines and one thousand soldiers, marching between Tampa Bay and Fort King, were ambushed on the Withlacoochee River by Osceola and his warriors, who held them there ten days. Running out of provisions and forced to kill their horses for food, they were finally reinforced by General Clinch. The Seminoles withdrew only after Osceola had been shot in the arm.

Another command was enticed into a swamp near Lake Okeechobee. When the men were immersed in a thick growth of saw grass five feet high and wading knee-deep in mud and water, Osceola attacked. Twenty-six whites were killed and 112 wounded; Osceola lost only 10 warriors.

Osceola took two more wives to comfort him for the loss of Checho-ter. They accompanied him on his marches as did the wives of the other warriors, some of them abandoning their children to fight beside the men.

So the game of hide-and-seek continued until still another army commander, General Thomas S. Jesup, was sent to end it. He and Chief Jumper drew up another treaty at Camp Dade. They agreed that Negro slaves of the Seminoles would be allowed to accompany them to the West, and that a month later they all were to assemble at Tampa Bay for deportation. Jesup was so sure of success that he had twenty-four transports ready to remove three thousand Seminoles. But Osceola refuted the agreement made by Jumper, and no Seminoles appeared.

Frustrated, Jesup wrote bitterly, "No Seminole proves false to his country, nor has a single instance ever occurred of a first-rate warrior having surrendered."

He ordered Colonel Zachary Taylor with 1,050 soldiers to scour the country along the Kissimmee River and bring in Seminoles. Some 484 Indians were captured. Then Philip, chief of the St. John's River Band, was taken and imprisoned at St. Augustine.

A short time later Philip's son Cooacoochee, "The Wildcat," arrived under a flag of truce to see his father. He was put in irons, then released to carry a message to Osceola requesting him to come to a large peace parley with General Jesup. When Cooacoochee returned, he was imprisoned with his father.

Osceola debated a long time with his warriors as to whether he should attend the parley.

"How can we trust these white men?" they asked him. "They have betrayed us many times. They will again."

"General Jesup I do not know," Osceola answered thoughtfully. "Perhaps he is different, being a powerful man who has replaced all the others who have failed."

Then he learned that a large delegation of Cherokees would also attend the parley. "We are all troubled with the same disease. Cherokees, Creeks, Seminoles, Chickasaws, and Choctaws too. Let us all make one more attempt to come to terms with the government that would move us."

So that fall Osceola with a party of fifty-three Seminoles and sixteen Negroes set out for St. Augustine under a flag of truce to General Jesup's peace conference. Seven miles out of St. Augustine they made camp to await their call to enter the fort. It never came. Instead, they were suddenly surrounded by soldiers and taken prisoner.

General Jesup was delighted; in capturing Osceola, he had accomplished what all previous commanders had failed to do.

Chief John Ross, who headed the Cherokee delegation, was so shocked and mortified that he obtained permission to assure Osceola he had not been a party to this act of treachery. He then wrote a long, indignant letter to the secretary of war, saying, "I do hereby most solemnly protest against this unprecedented violation of that sacred rule . . . of treating with all due respect those who had ever presented themselves under a flag of truce."

A few nights later Cooacoochee, "The Wildcat," escaped from the fort. Before crawling through the hole in the wall he had dug, his father and Osceola had told him, "Carry news of our betrayal to all our people. No matter what happens to us, they must fight on."

Osceola and the other chiefs, Micanope, Philip, Co-e-harjo, and Yahaloochee (Little Cloud), with 116 warriors and 82 women and children, were then shipped on the Poinsett to Charleston, South Carolina, and imprisoned in Fort Moultrie, Georgia. That January,

1838, the famous artist George Catlin came to paint the portraits of the five chiefs.

Osceola became ill and could not finish the sittings. It was believed he was afflicted with chronic malaria aggravated by a sore throat; and the post surgeon, Dr. Weedon, was sent to attend him. But as Weedon was the brother-in-law of General Wiley Thompson, Osceola refused to see him, accepting only the care of a trusted Seminole. Dressing in his ceremonial costume, the dying man lay on the floor in front of the fire with his two wives and two children beside him.

Observing that he was in "great distress of mind," Catlin wrote: "The papers say that his disease was an affection of the throat, but grief and mortification had their share in bringing him to his end. . . . His bold spirit took its flight on the evening of January 30."

Osceola had been imprisoned scarcely three months and was only thirty-five years old. Yet his impassioned resistance encouraged the Seminoles to fight on for another four years in a war that cost the government fifteen hundred American lives and $20 million. Most of the Seminoles were then removed to Indian Territory with the other four Civilized Tribes. Today, living in the depths of the Florida Everglades, there are still small bands whose forefathers never surrendered.

Mangas Coloradas

A WIDE STRIP from the Rio Grande to the Colorado running across
southern New Mexico and Arizona in the United States, and northern
Chihuahua and Sonora in Mexico — this was Apacheria, the country
of the Apaches. A sun-stricken desert of parched rock mountains,
forests of giant saguaro cactus, alkali flats, and wastes of sand where
water holes were few and springs were far apart.

Why the Apaches picked such a forbidding homeland no one
knows. They were an Athabascan-speaking people who had migrated
southward from Lake Athabasca in Canada. Arriving in the Southwest
perhaps as late as the seventeenth century, they were given the name
of *Apache* (or Enemy) by the Pueblos. But while part of them, the
Apaches de Navaju (or Navajos), remained in Pueblo country, the rest
of them continued south to claim all Apacheria.

In this immense area, the tribe split into many groups: the Mim-
breños along the Mimbres River in southwest New Mexico, the
Jicarillas to the north, the Warm Springs and Mescaleros to the east,
and the Coyoteros and Chiricahuas to the west in Arizona.

Mangas Coloradas was a Mimbres Apache, a Mimbreño. As a boy
he had been given the name of Dasoda-hee or simply Don-Ha,
"He-Who-Just-Sits-There," because he always sat listening to the
words of his elders after other boys had gone to bed. Nevertheless, he
soon learned what a man should know in order to be master of such a
large domain. He was never taught to ride a horse. He was simply
placed with a herd and expected within a few days to know the strength
and tricks of every horse. If one were killed under him, he knew how

to cut up the carcass and utilize every bit of hide, flesh, and sinew. He learned the desert plants, the art of tracking and of emptying his mind when he was concealing himself, and how to find underground water.

"You will soon do that which will make a warrior name for you," suggested Soldado Fiero, the chief.

"The time will come," said Don-Ha, just sitting there.

He went on raids, many raids. For the Apaches held a great contempt for those who raised corn and herded sheep; they lived by plundering the settlements of the Nakai-yes, the Mexicans. Toughened to unbelievable endurance, able to ride hundreds of miles with a bit of jerky and a greasy intestine filled with drinking water slung over their shoulders, they raided Ariape, the former capital of Sonora, Ures the present capital, and Hermosillo the future capital. Even Ciudad Chihuahua, the capital of the state of Chihuahua, suffered frequent losses of men, women, and children taken as captives, as well as horses, mules, and plunder. To be sure, a few of the Apaches left their heads to be mounted above the city gates. What did that matter? *"La raza que sabe morir,"* Soldado Fiero told Don-Ha, pointing out the drying head of an old friend killed during one raid. "We are the race that knows how to die!"

Mangas Coloradas, or Don-Ha, was different from most Apaches. While they were generally small of build, he was a tall, powerfully built man with a massive head. And instead of performing a feat of daring to make a new name for himself, he still preferred to sit quietly thinking.

"Action is useless unless it is the fruit of thought," he would say. "The heart, the mind, the time must work together. My day will come."

It came when he captured a young Mexican girl in a pack train traveling to Janos in Chihuahua. Her name was Ana, and she pleased him. He announced she would be his third wife.

His declaration displeased his people, for it was their custom to make slaves of such captives. Lost Pony, brother of Mangas Coloradas's first wife, was angry. "You would bring shame upon my sister by making this Mexican girl a wife instead of a slave?"

Mangas Coloradas nodded gravely.

"Then you will be ready tomorrow morning?" asked Lost Pony.

"I will be ready," answered Mangas Coloradas.

The next morning in open combat, in a circle of massed Apaches, Mangas Coloradas killed Lost Pony with his knife.

That evening, while nursing his own knife cuts, he was challenged to another combat by Pindah, brother of the second wife of Mangas Coloradas. The following morning, within the same ring of watchers, he killed Pindah. His own arms covered with blood, he walked to Ana on the edge of the circle and slipped them through a Mexican red flannel undershirt she was holding.

It was all over — his wives' jealousy, the family feuds, his tribe's resentment. "La-choy Ko-kun-noste — Mangas Coloradas — 'Red Sleeves'!" the people shouted. He had made his new name — a name that was soon to be known and feared from the Rio Grande to the Colorado. Ana always pleased him. She had a thatched brush house, a wickiup of her own; and eventually she bore him three daughters.

Now came those events which were to make Mangas Coloradas a chief. For many years the Mexicans had been working some copper mines at Santa Rita del Cobre nearby and carrying the ore down to Chihuahua and Sonora in *conductas* of mule trains. Juan José, an Apache chief, permitted them to do this provided the Mexican *conductas* did not leave Santa Rita without his permission. The Mexicans were irked at these restrictions and angered by the continued Apache raids. The junta of Chihuahua finally passed a *proyecto de guerra*, a bill of war against the Apaches, offering a bounty of $100 for the scalp of every Apache man, $50 for that of a woman, and $25 for that of a child.

During this time, the American trappers came into the country. One of them, James Johnson, suggested to the *alcalde*, or mayor, of Santa Rita a way to collect bounties on a number of Apache scalps at one time, avoiding all risk to themselves. Accordingly, they invited Juan José and a large crowd of Apaches to a feast and to meet the new *Americanos*.

Mangas Coloradas smelled trouble, but he went, seating himself at the edge of the crowd. Everybody was dressed in their finest: the unarmed warriors with carefully painted faces, the women in beads and fringed buckskin, the babies sewed in their cradleboards. There was plenty of *mescal*, hot chunks of beef from the fire, tortillas, and chile. Señor Johnson and the white *Americanos* laughed and talked. "Los Goddamies," Mangas Coloradas called them. At the end of the feast, bags of grain were piled in the center of the plaza; and the Apaches were invited to help themselves. As the women rushed forward to gather corn in their skirts, Mangas Coloradas noticed Señor Johnson. The Goddamie walked to a big black iron object pointed at the crowd, and touched it with the lighted *cigarillo* in his hand.

Instantly the howitzer belched forth fire and smoke, pouring its charge of bullets, slugs, and nails into the gathered guests. And now into this bloody mess of writhing arms and legs, a mass butchery of unarmed men, women, and children, rushed the Goddamies and Mexicans to finish off the wounded and to collect their scalps.

Mangas Coloradas, escaping, fled back to camp. Juan José was dead; Soldado Fiero had been killed in a raid in Mexico. Proclaiming himself chief, Mangas Coloradas quickly appointed new leaders: Delgadito, Cuchillo Negro (Black Knife), Victorio, and Colletto Amarillo (Yellow Tail). To them he gave precise orders.

"Attack and kill every member of every *conducta* on the way to Chihuahua and Sonora," he said. "Surprise and kill every one of the other American trapping parties in the country. Burn wagons and goods. Cover ashes with dirt. Leave no sign they ever lived. Do not spare the horses when you ride back."

Then began the siege of Santa Rita. None of the miners ever saw their besiegers. They only knew that when one of them set foot outside the village, he was killed by an arrow from an invisible foe. Weeks passed. Food gave out. Starving and cut off from the world, the whole population began a desperate march on foot to Janos, the nearest military post in Chihuahua. Only then did Mangas and his Apaches attack. They showed no mercy. Of the three to four hundred people, only a half dozen reached Janos with news of the massacre.

It seemed for a time the Apaches had got rid of their enemies. For the Americans had won a war with the Mexicans and proclaimed a wide strip of Apacheria from the Rio Grande to the Colorado as the Territory of New Mexico of the United States. Then more God-damies came, settling near Santa Rita at Pinos Altos, where they had discovered gold. Controlling his thoughts, for days Mangas Coloradas watched from the hills. That is what makes a chief. Never to act hastily in anger, but to weigh all things. Finally, out of his deep meditation came the conclusion. He rose and walked down to talk to the digging white men.

He had come to tell them that in a secret place far over the mountains there was much of this yellow iron they sought. He would show it to them and thus rid his country of them. But the gleam in their eyes, the greed on their bearded faces, their loud laughs spoke a warning to his heart.

"So you'll show us the gold, eh chief?"

Mangas Coloradas rose. "This day, no. Maybe soon."

Suddenly the butt of a pistol cracked over his head and darkness came. When it lifted, he found his hands tied and a rope lifting him to his toes. The big Goddamie was laughing. "Big old bull, ain't he? Tryin' to give us a cock-and-bull story like that! Come on, boys! Let's teach him a lesson!"

Then came slashing blows from rope and strap. Fighting back the blackness, he counted them carefully. When the men released him, his legs were weak but his will was strong. He did not fall till he was out of sight. Then he crawled all night, and hid himself and his disgrace until his back was healed.

"Ten blows four times, and ten lives shall pay for each blow!" he vowed.

He planned carefully the marriages of his three daughters by Ana. One he gave to the chief of Chiricahuas, Cochise; another to Co-si-to of the Coyoteros; and the third to Kutu-hala of the White Mountain Apaches. It was well he bound himself by blood to these tribes, for he needed their help to stop the increasing flow of Americans. Not only wagon trains of settlers were coming in, but the Butterfield mail stage was running across Apacheria from El Paso del Norte on the Rio Grande to Fort Yuma on the Colorado along the southern route to California.

And now appeared the Chiricahua Apache chief Cochise, to talk to him alone in a small glade. "I come to ask the help of our people's greatest war chief," he said.

"Empty your heart," Mangas Coloradas told the younger man. Cochise spoke at length. The Butterfield stagecoaches passed through the Chiricahua Mountains at Apache Pass. Here the white man maintained a stage station and paid the Chiricahuas to keep it supplied with wood in return for allowing the stages to pass unmolested.

"It was thus you stopped our enemies?" asked Mangas Coloradas.

"It was then I was betrayed," answered Cochise. A band of Coyoteros had burned a white man's ranch house and captured a small boy. Hearing of this, a young shavetail from Fort Buchanan, Lieutenant George Bascom, rode with a detachment to Apache Pass. Under a white flag of truce he invited Cochise with his son, brother, and two nephews for a talk. Regarding all Indians as treacherous savages, Bascom ordered Cochise to give up the white boy. Cochise denied the charges that his Chiricahuas were guilty, and was put under arrest. That night he slashed his way out of the tent. Gathering his warriors, he attacked a wagon train, killing eight men and capturing six prisoners. These he offered to exchange for the Apache prisoners. Young Lieutenant Bascom refused, and hanged his Apache prisoners. That night Cochise tortured his own prisoners to death, tying them upside down to the wheels of a wagon and burning them. "Thus were we betrayed under a flag of truce," finished Cochise. "Now I have said it all." In answer Mangas Coloradas stood up and slipped the shirt off his back, revealing for the first time to another its scarred ridges and long welts.

"I have seen nothing," said Cochise, "but I will carry your answer back to my people."

To Cadete, the chief of the Mescaleros, Mangas Coloradas sent word, and to all chiefs of all the other Apache bands. Under him they all united in one great effort to drive the invaders from their land. Not only did ten American lives pay for each of the ten blows four times that had slashed the back of Mangas Coloradas, but there was hardly a campsite along the southern route that did not show human bones and burnt remnants of wagons and boxes.

Reported the *Arizonian* newspaper in August 1861:

> We are hemmed in on all sides by the unrelenting Apache. Within six months, nine-tenths of the whole male population have been killed off, and every ranch, farm, and mine in the country has been abandoned in consequence.

Despite the outbreak of the Civil War, the United States government in 1862 dispatched Colonel James H. Carleton with a small army of fourteen hundred men from Los Angeles, California, to open and keep open the southern route. Two months later his advance guard of three hundred men under Captain Thomas Roberts reached Apache Pass. Mangas Coloradas and his warriors were waiting on both sides of the deep gorge below the springs. As the Bluecoats crawled up the canyon, the Indians opened fire. Roberts brought up two mountain howitzers, and the battle of Apache Pass began. The roars of the howitzers were punctuated by the shrill cries of the Apaches and the sharp cracks of their muskets. There was a swarm of maddened horses. Knives and bayonets flashed in the sun. Then after four hours of fighting there came a sudden silence.

When the main body of the California Column arrived, not an

Apache was to be seen. What had happened?

Badly wounded, Mangas Coloradas had been shot off his horse. In tribute to their great leader, the Apaches rallied around him and carried him in a litter across the desolate plain of Chihuahua to Janos. It was a remote little town with an old cathedral and a tiny presidio surrounding a round watchtower. The Apaches had raided it often. Now the warriors encircled the presidio and sat watching as Mangas Coloradas was carried inside to a Mexican doctor.

"You make him well. *Bueno!* We go!" they said. "He die, everybody die!"

Was it their threats, the great chief's constitution, or the prayers of the priest and people of Janos that pulled Mangas Coloradas through? The bullet was extracted, and he lived.

Back at Apache Pass, Carleton left a detachment to build Fort Bowie and continued his march. On his way he found the charred bones of nine white men whom the Apaches had burned at the stake. Nor had Mangas Coloradas forgotten Pinos Altos. His warriors had besieged it, allowing no one to leave. A rescue force arriving at the mining settlement found all the families starving. They had been living on roots, and several of them had gone insane.

In 1863 the Territory of Arizona was created, and Americans began swarming in to establish towns, ranches, and mines. Mangas Coloradas, seventy years old, knew he had reached the end of his trail.

Who could take his place? Trusted Victorio would become the leading chief, but he would not last long. Cochise was a good chief, but as a friend of the whites he had been betrayed; and again he would be their friend and be betrayed. Cadete would fight to the death, yet did not have the wisdom to make him chief of all. The young renegade Geronimo, "The Yawner," was not dependable enough to ever become a true chief; he depended only upon his personal bravery as an independent warrior. What, thought Mangas Coloradas, could he do now to consolidate and save his people?

According to the noted Arizona historian Lawrence Clark Powell,

Mangas Coloradas was treacherously delivered to the American troops by John W. ("Jack") Swilling, who founded Phoenix. Swilling, known as a tricky adventurer, was later indicted for the holdup of the Wickenburg stage, and died in the Yuma jail while awaiting trial.

Will Levington Comfort, in his sympathetic, novelized biography of the great Apache chief, gives another version. He recounts that Mangas Coloradas walked under a white flag of truce to the white soldiers' camp with the hope of keeping his people from being exterminated.

Made prisoner, he was taken before Colonel J. J. West, commander of Fort McLane. "I came to talk of peace," Mangas Coloradas told him. "I speak for all my people — every tribe, every band, every Apache everywhere. During war we give no quarter, in peace we do not betray our word. Nevermore, if you agree, will any Apache raise his hand against one of your people."

"Mangas Coloradas, the time for talking peace is over," the colonel said sternly. "I have followed your trail of burned bodies for five hundred miles. Now at last you're our prisoner. If you make the slightest move to escape, you will be shot. Do you understand?"

He turned from the interpreter to the guards and spoke in a lower voice. Mangas Coloradas did not understand what he said, but he knew what he meant.

That evening he sat by a fire outside, watching the guards heating the tips of their bayonets, and glimpsing the flash of rifles in the brush beyond. One of the guards flipped red sparks over the old chief's naked body.

"Am I a child to be played with?" Mangas Coloradas asked quietly.

The soldiers laughed. "Look at the size of him! Ever see such a brute? He's got the shanks of a mule!"

The bayonets were glowing red now, and the men kept touching them to his arms and legs. He did not flinch. Death comes in many ways, and torture is only one of them. "*¡La raza de bronce que sabe morir!*": "The bronze race that knows how to die!"

The two guards raised their rifles. Others were in the brush, and their rifles were still glinting. Suddenly the reddened bayonets were held across his belly. Mangas Coloradas's mind and heart did not flinch even then, but the reflex of his muscles unbent his body. That drew the fire of the rifles upon him, those from the guards and those from the soldiers waiting in the bush. It was reported that he had been killed while attempting to escape.

What a vivid scene Will Levington Comfort has reconstructed! It is not certain that next morning Mangas Coloradas was scalped by a man who wanted his lustrous black hair. But it is true that his head was later cut off and shipped to the Smithsonian, which then sold it to a phrenologist named O. S. Fowler.

Yet it was one of his enemies, Captain John C. Cremony, who wrote his epitaph:

> He was the greatest and most talented Apache of the nineteenth
> century. . . . His sagacious counsels partook more of the character
> of wide and enlightened leadership than those of any other Indian
> of modern times. . . . He found means to collect and keep together,
> for weeks at a time, large bodies of savages, such as none of his
> predecessors could assemble and feed . . . and taught them to
> comprehend the value of unity and collective strength. . . . Take
> him all in all, he exercised influence never equalled by any other
> savage of our time.

MANULITO.   NAV

Manuelito

Manuelito, a fine-looking young Navajo wearing a woolen shoulder blanket, knee-high deerskin moccasins, and muslin pantaloons, looked about him as he sat on his horse that September morning in 1849. Around him in a great semicircle sat more Navajo horsemen with their head chief, Narbona, Manuelito's father-in-law. Narbona was a rheumatic old man of eighty wrapped in a striped chief blanket. He was usually carried in a litter, but Manuelito had boosted him on a horse for this great occasion.

Before them stood James S. Calhoun, the first American territorial Indian agent, later territorial governor of New Mexico, and hook-nosed Colonel John M. Washington with an escort of 175 soldiers who had marched from Santa Fe, over Washington Pass, to this remote spot near Two Grey Hills to draw up a treaty with the Navajos.

Calhoun began the peace talk: "The United States has won its war with Mexico, and now all this land of New Mexico belongs to the Americans. We want to make peace with you. To make a treaty you must surrender all your American, Mexican, and Indian captives, and all the cattle and sheep you have stolen. Also you must not molest American wagon trains which pass through your country. In return, the United States will keep the peace and make you presents of trade goods."

Narbona was perplexed because both Americans and Mexicans kept Navajo captives as slaves. But he agreed to surrender 130 sheep his men had stolen. At this moment a Mexican in Washington's command recognized one of the Navajos' horses. It had been stolen from him, and he demanded it back.

The Navajo refused: "Of course I stole it a long time ago, according to custom, but this Mexican has been afraid to claim it. Does he need all these Bluecoats to get his horse back now?"

"Seize that horse!" ordered Colonel Washington.

As the Mexican stepped forward, Manuelito gave a high-pitched yell. The Navajos wheeled their mounts. What happened then Manuelito never forgot. There was a volley of shots. Chief Narbona and six Navajo warriors fell dead. Then sounded three bursts of artillery, and all around him the Navajos raced for safety.

"A fine peace treaty!" he yelled. "The Americans have a lot to teach us!"

He spoke truly without knowing it, for the distinguishing trait of the Navajos was their remarkable adaptativeness; they learned from all their enemies. Migrating from the north with their Athabascan cousins, the Apaches, they had stayed here in northern New Mexico and Arizona. From the Pueblos, the oldest residents, they had learned to plant corn, squash, beans, and tobacco. Settling down, they developed their own unique style of home: a large *hogan* of logs, octagonal in shape, with the door always facing east. Inside, a fire was built in the center of the floor, the smoke escaping through a hole in the roof.

Later from the Spanish settlers they obtained sheep and horses. The sheep provided them with a steady supply of meat and wool with which they wove blankets to replace their skin clothing. With horses they could travel far and quickly. Soon they had spread from the Chama River almost to the Grand Canyon. This was plateau country, seas of green sage billowing into swells of scrub cedar, rising into ranges of pine and spruce, and falling away into immense canyons and deep chasms.

From this homeland Manuelito also would ride with a small band to raid the adobe towns of the Pueblos and of the Mexicans, running off horses and sheep, and carrying back women for slaves. Mexican *hacendados* and army officers would strike back, returning with re-captured stock and Navajo women for slaves. Yet they could not stop the continuing raids of the Navajos. Not even the capital of New Mexico, Santa Fe, was safe from their attacks.

Manuelito's favorite horse was a pinto fast and clever as a racer snake. Manuelito called him Racer. During one of his raids, the Navajos ran into a stray band of Comanches, and Manuelito was shot. His brother, Cayatanita, dashed in, lifted Manuelito to his own horse, and carried him to safety.

The bullet had not gone through his body. It had to be dug out. The man selected to perform this operation was Herrero Delgadito, "Thin Smith," a blacksmith who had learned how to make iron horse bits from the Mexicans. Manuelito recovered, but always carried a round scar under his right breast. The Americans, not yet knowing his right name, called him Pistol Hole.

They were soon to learn it, for the Navajos continued their raids. "This has got to stop!" Colonel Sumner told his officers of the First Dragoons. "During the last four years they've stolen from the Rio Grande villages 12,000 mules, 7,000 horses, 31,000 cattle, and 450,000 sheep! And another thing. These Navajos are sitting right on the new thirty-fifth parallel route to California."

"What do you propose, Colonel?"

"To establish a fort just south of Canyon de Chelly, the heart of Navajo country!" he answered tersely. "If this post doesn't put a stop to their depredations, nothing will do it but their complete extermi-nation!"

The site he selected was a small grassy meadow overlooked by the walls of Canyon Bonito. The Navajos called it Meadow Between Rocks. Erecting a rectangle of adobe and log buildings, with a parade ground and a flagpole in the center, the colonel named it Fort Defiance. The soldiers he left there called it Hell's Gate, "the loneliest corner in the United States."

Ganado Mucho, "Many Cattle," who owned large flocks and

herds and had a *hogan* for each of his many wives, wanted to make peace. So did Long Earrings, often called Many Buttons because he had adopted Mexican knee breeches trimmed with silver buttons.

Around a fire at night Manuelito in his buckskin leggings and bright blanket made fun of these peace talkers: "They are rich and fat and lazy! They want peace. We want our beautiful land. We want to drive out these Americans who would steal it from us. We want war!" Other chiefs agreed with him: crafty old Sarcillo Largo, Herrero Delgadito, and Hosteen Dagai, or "Mr. Whiskers," usually known by his Spanish name of Barboncito.

So more peace treaties were made and ignored. More expeditions of Bluecoats marched out from the fort to conquer the Navajos. One of them with 55 guides marched 349 miles and killed only 10 Navajos. Manuelito was too smart; he never let a warrior be seen. Still he kept running off the herd of cattle at Fort Defiance and attacking wagon trains passing by.

The climax came one April dawn in 1860. Major Sheppard, the fort commander, was awakened by the shrill war whoops of two thousand Navajos. Jumping out of bed, he rushed from his quarters. "Sound the 'Call to Arms'!" he yelled to his bugler. Clothes half on, clutching their rifles, men poured out of their barracks into the parade ground. "Form companies!" And now in the paling light began the defense of Hell's Gate.

Company E was dispatched to the magazine and the stables on the southwest corner to quiet the screaming, plunging horses. Company C charged to the west side and was driven back by a shower of arrows. Company B took position on the east side, firing at the Navajos on the cliffs above. With rifles against arrows and a few old muskets, the troops gradually drove back their attackers. When daylight came, Sheppard massed all three companies and led them up the hill.

The Navajos had retreated, leaving only one dead warrior whose faithful pony refused to move from his side. The soldiers killed it where it stood vigil.

Manuelito and other war chiefs were never able again to mass the Navajos in one great effort to drive out the intruders. The tribe was divided into forty-three clans living far apart in their immense wilderness, and it was difficult to get them together.

The Americans faced the same problem in their attempts to defeat the Navajos. Two years later General Carleton — who had opened up the southern route across Apacheria — took steps to solve it. Under what was called his Black Flag Policy, he established in 1862 the Bosque Redondo Reservation, forty miles square, in southeastern New Mexico, with Fort Sumner in its center. In this vast prison camp he proposed to confine all Indians that could be rounded up in a great hunt.

A large army was organized; so many private citizens volunteered to join the hunt for the hated Navajos that the governor of New Mexico was forced to call them off by proclamation. Kit Carson, the famous Indian scout, was placed in charge. He began the campaign in July, enlisting Utes as guides, and requesting that they be allowed to keep the Navajo women and children they captured as slaves. Next he moved into the Hopi village of Oraibi, demanding more guides. The Hopis refused. Carson promptly bound the head chief in ropes and took him prisoner. Then the scout advanced slowly northward.

Manuelito became alarmed. "What kind of a war is this? The Rope Thrower boasts every living Navajo will be killed or made prisoner, yet he will fight no battles!"

It was true. Carson, "The Rope Thrower," fought no battles. He simply burnt every patch of corn, ran in every band of sheep, and relentlessly tracked down every family with his Ute scouts. Manuelito and his people, armed only with bows and arrows, and a few guns for which they had no more powder and lead, kept retreating northward. Without sheep or corn, they lived on roots and grass seeds, afraid to make a fire lest the soldiers see the smoke.

By winter most of the Navajos had reached their stronghold,

Canyon de Chelly, three gorges slashed a thousand feet deep into the mile-high plateau. High in the canyon walls were hundreds of ancient cliff dwellings reached by hand and toe holds cut into the rock, and on the floor of the canyon grew a thousand or more stunted peach trees. "Here we will be safe," the people told one another.

"Here you will be caught," Manuelito told them; and with a small band of refugees he continued on to hide in the mountains.

In January Kit Carson's troops trapped the Navajos in the canyon. Detachments blocked all paths of escape and cut down the peach trees. A foot of snow fell. Intense cold set in. Huddling in their icy caves without wood for fires, and without even the bark of the peach trees for food, the Navajos faced death, starvation, or capture. One at a time they began to surrender.

In March they began their Long Walk to captivity at Bosque Redondo, 300 miles away — 7,353 people, with wagons carrying the aged, wounded, and children, trudging across land as desolate and empty as their hearts.

New Mexico was joyous. Bells rang in Santa Fe, and the governor proclaimed a day of thanksgiving for their defeat.

All that year stray bands were rounded up or surrendered. Among the last to be sent to Bosque Redondo was Manuelito and his little group. To him "Sweet Carletonia," as that great concentration camp was called, was an appalling sight. It now contained 8,500 Navajos and some 400 Mescalero Apaches. The land was a barren patch of mesquite without wood and fresh water. The prisoners lived in brush shelters or in pits dug in the ground. Kiowas and Comanches ran off their few sheep. The alkaline water sickened them. They quarreled with the Mescaleros. Corrupt government officials, army officers, and Indian agents stole supplies and beef sent in as rations. When they were issued the meat of diseased cattle, many prisoners died. Chief Barboncito and Ganado Blanco escaped, but Blanco was killed and Barboncito recaptured by pursuing cavalrymen.

"Oh, for the sacred mountains of our beautiful homeland!" the people cried to Manuelito. "What do you say now?"

Manuelito said nothing. He was chipping arrowheads for which he had no shafts.

General Carleton regarded the place as a model prisoners' camp. He insisted, "The Indians on the reservation are the happiest people I have ever seen." From St. Louis he ordered a thousand-pound bell "to be used as a signal for hours of labor and repose for the Indians." Its cost was paid out of the little money the Navajos made by selling straw to the cavalry. Then he put the men to work digging thirty miles of irrigation ditches and planting 2,800 acres to corn and wheat. Every crop for three years was a failure. To reduce the cost of feeding the Navajos to twelve cents per head a day, each prisoner was given only a pound of beef and a pound of corn with a pinch of salt.

News of the disgraceful concentration camp, which already had cost the government $10 million, reached Congress. General William Tecumseh Sherman, who had made the famous march to the sea through Georgia, and Peace Commissioner S. F. Tappas were sent to determine what could be done with these starving, heartbroken Navajos. The decision was to return them to their homeland, "which is as far out of the way of the whites and of our future possible wants as possible."

So in 1868 a treaty was drawn up and signed by 12 Navajo chiefs, including Manuelito, Barboncito, and Ganado Mucho. Then the remaining 7,111 Navajos were marched back home in a procession ten miles long. At Window Rock they were issued two sheep and goats apiece. The Navajos then strode off into the trackless wilderness, where they were expected to die off quickly with no embarrassment to the white people.

"What does it matter that we have no clothes, no tools, no guns, no food!" cried Manuelito. "We are home at last!"

And now began their fight for survival. "It is not the first time," Manuelito counseled. "Kill your two sheep and goats and then starve. Multiply them and live to grow into a mighty nation."

He spoke with authority, for he was chief of the east side of the mountains. Ganado Mucho had gone back to his grasslands near Ganado, where he was chief on the west side of the mountains. Barboncito, the third head chief, lived near Fort Defiance, which was the headquarters of the government agency. Some of the Navajos began again to steal cattle and sheep in order to increase their stock. To stop it, the government organized a large force of Navajo scouts with Manuelito in charge.

"Our war chief has now become a peace chief!" some of the people accused him. "What has happened to you?"

"This is our reservation now by treaty," he told them sternly. "Let us not break our word or we may lose it." The land. He began to fight for it now by peaceful means as he had fought for it with bow and arrows. With other chiefs he went to Washington and, while there, protested that surveyors were taking Navajo land.

One of the officials explained. The surveyors were laying out a route for a railroad, the Atlantic and Pacific Railway. It was the law that every other section of 640 acres for a 40-mile strip on each side of the tracks was to be given to the railroad company.

"But that is our land by treaty," protested Manuelito. "If you take it, you must give us more in place of it. We are keeping our word. The government must keep its word, too."

So the government enlarged the Navajo Reservation to an eventual 25,000 square miles, completely enclosing the small 4,000-square-mile Hopi Reservation which had been established in 1882.

Before long, gangs of laborers began to lay the rails. Many Navajos were hired to help with unskilled work. This was good. They learned how to fashion scrap iron into sheep-shearing knives and arrowheads. Also they were given their first wheeled boxes. Not knowing how to use them, the men broke them up to get the iron.

"This is not right!" Manuelito cautioned. "We learned many things in the old days from the Pueblos, from the Spanish, the Mexicans. Now we must learn new things from the Americans."

To teach them, he learned to harness horses to his own wagon and began hauling supplies from the railroad junction to Fort Manuelito.

The Navajos were beginning to prosper now. With iron they could forge tools for making beautiful bracelets, earrings, and necklaces out of melted-down American silver dollars and Mexican pesos. Their few sheep had multiplied into great flocks producing thousands of pounds of wool. Most of this they hauled in their wagons to the new trading capital of Gallup. The women resumed their weaving of blankets, which brought good prices everywhere.

Still Manuelito was not satisfied. According to the treaty he signed, the government promised to provide a school for every thirty Navajo children. Yet ten years later there was only one school, which had but eleven pupils; and not a single Navajo on the reservation could read and write. One reason for this violation of the treaty was that the Navajos were spread out over an immense wilderness without roads. Another was that children's parents wanted them to herd sheep instead of wasting time in a white man's school.

Manuelito set a good example by sending his own two sons to a new away-school for Indians established at Carlisle, Pennsylvania.

"My sons," he told them when they got on the train, "when I was your age I was fighting the Americans with bow and arrows. Now both of us have changed, Americans and Navajos. I am no longer a war chief, but a peace chief. The Americans have many things which we must have in order to grow into a great people. To get them we must learn to read and write. So work hard in school that you may come back as peace chiefs and teach others."

Tragically, one son died of tuberculosis, and the other came home an invalid. Manuelito took to drink and became a pathetic, dissolute old man. Yet in his wasting frame he still embodied the unique genius of his people, the adaptiveness of the Navajo. Drunk as he usually was, he kept counseling young men as he had his own sons. He was determined to find one to serve as a bridge between the old way of life and the new.

The bridge he found was Kiilchii (Red Boy) — Henry Chee Dodge — who as a baby was said to have been taken on the Long Walk to Bosque Redondo. Of all their talks, Chee Dodge always remembered best Manuelito's advice just before he died in 1894: "My grandchild, the whites have many things which we Navajos need. But we cannot get them. It is as though the whites were in a grassy canyon and there they have wagons, plows, and plenty of food. We Navajo are on the dry mesa. We can hear them talking, but we cannot get to them. My grandchild, education is the ladder. Tell our people to take it."

Chee Dodge slowly climbed up that ladder himself before telling others how. He became the first Navajo to read and write English, a partner in a large trading company, and an influential businessman who knew both American and Navajo ways. He was then elected the first chairman of the modern Navajo Tribal Council in 1923, and then two times more.

These were the years of the Navajos' rise to power, wealth, and glory. Governed by an elected chairman and 74 members of a tribal council, this "Nation within a Nation" had increased to a population of more than 100,000 living on a reservation of 25,000 square miles, the largest in the United States.

As the saying goes, all that goes up comes down. The climax of its history didn't last. Causes within and outside contributed to its fall: rivalry between this powerful Navajo Nation and the small Hopi Nation which had fallen under the complete control of the federal government's Bureau of Indian Affairs; and the discovery of immense deposits of coal in Black Mesa, owned by both tribes, and its strip-mining by a corporate conglomerate given its lease by the government. Indications of more coal and mineral deposits within the Hopi Reservation resulted in a legal maze worked to advantage by the Hopi lawyer, abetted by the federal government. A 300-mile barbed wire fence was built to divide the so-called joint-use area, the Hopi side containing 11,000 Navajos and the Navajo side only 100 Hopis. The enforced relocation of the Navajos with their sheep, homes, graves, and shrines has been a failure. Still going on, it is being blocked by 350 families at Big Mountain. Their refusal to move from their sacred homeland is being spearheaded by the women.

A telling footnote to the Navajos' fall from grace was the conviction in two 1990 tribal trials of the Navajo tribal chairman of that time for misuse of tribal funds, bribery, fraud, and profiting ; he currently faces trial under two federal indictments.

Irataba

THE MOHAVES WERE GREAT DREAMERS of dreams, dreamers who believed in their dreams. And of all their dreams, that of Irataba which came true and betrayed him was the saddest.

Irataba was only a boy, and his world was small. For the Mohaves lived on the left bank of the Colorado River just below the sharp-pointed crags, or *picachos*, called The Needles. Across the river to the west stretched the vast Mohave Desert, where the boy seldom ventured. In the crinkled desert mountains to the east he hunted rabbits and deer, becoming skillful with his bow and arrows. From above he could see to the north where the mighty red river swirled out of the Grand Canyon and around the big bend to pour on south through narrow Mohave Canyon.

In the spring the river was swelled to a raging torrent by melting snows in the high mountains. Then, in the flooded bottomlands, Irataba would help to plant corn, melons, beans, and pumpkins. In the blazing heat of summer he would plaster his head and naked body with mud to keep away insects, and laze in the shade of a willow-thatched hut, or *ramada*. When the sinking sun grew red enough to stain even redder the red Colorado, he bathed in its muddy flow and watched the teal and long-legged white herons in the tules. The nights were desert nights, and the stars hung bright and low. They were nights to dream. And on such a night he dreamed he would be the mighty chief of all the Mohaves.

"But let me warn you," his Dream Person told him, "you will see new things and strange things that no other Mohave has ever seen.

And you must never be afraid of them, new and strange as they may seem. Thus only can you become a mighty chief."

Irataba remembered this as he grew up, becoming almost as big as Cairook, the chief. All the Mohaves were of gigantic build and strength, and Cairook was the largest. He stood nearly six and a half feet tall on his bare feet. His powerful naked body was covered only by a breechclout. Feathers from swans, herons, and vultures decorated his long hair. And when he went to war, he brandished the weapon which made the Mohaves feared all along the river — a huge war club shaped like a potato masher.

The Mohaves went often to war against the Chemehuevis who came upriver to steal their corn, pumpkins, and melons; the Paiutes who crept down across the great desert at night; or the Conina people, small bands of Walapais, Yavapais, and Havasupais who roamed the rocky plateau. Cairook always arranged his warriors in the same battle formation — the men with bows and arrows in front to keep the enemy at bay until he and his clubbers behind could get close enough to swing their mighty war clubs. Then the Mohaves advanced on foot, shooting their arrows and closing in to club bodies and smash heads like ripe pumpkins until the enemy fled.

"*Ahotka!* Good!" the Mohaves would shout in victory. "Thus are we masters of the river!" And they would return to their valley to laze in the sun and dream under the desert stars.

Irataba was a full-grown man and Cairook's most trusted sub-chief when in 1849 the new and strange things began to appear, as foretold by his dreams. There arrived from downriver a large party of white men with horses and mules and two huge boxes that rolled over the ground. The interpreter explained their presence to the several hundred Mohaves gathered around the strangers. The boxes on wheels were wagons; and the chiefs, Lieutenant Amiel Whipple and Lieutenant J. C. Ives, were surveying a route for many more wagons that some day would travel to the Great Water to the west. If this seemed strange, another chief pulled out a tooth from his mouth and put it back again.

"The white chiefs need the help of the Mohaves," concluded the interpreter. "Will you help them across the river?"

Irataba and other strong swimmers carried a rope to the opposite bank and with it hauled over the packs on a rubber pontoon. Then they towed across the river with two wagons, and drove across the horses and mules.

"And now we need brave Mohaves to lead us across the desert," announced the interpreter. "There will be presents for them."

So Cairook and Irataba guided the survey party across the waterless desert, through the country of the Paiutes, to the Old Spanish Trail from Nevada to southern California. "I will remember my friend," Lieutenant Ives said to Irataba as they parted. "You have been a great help to us white people."

Some years later another big party of white men came from the East. It was lead by E. F. Beale, who was establishing a direct road along the thirty-fifth parallel from the Rio Grande to the Colorado. The easy ford he found here he named Beale's Crossing. Again Irataba helped to ferry the party across the river so it could continue on to California.

Then suddenly that winter appeared a preposterous sight. A watcher had been posted high on the cliff wall of the canyon downriver, and his warning signal, a thin column of smoke, was seen by all Mohaves. Now they came running from their *rancherias* to crowd on the bank of the river — the huge men in their breechclouts, the short, heavy-breasted women wearing short skirts made of bark, the naked children. All watched an immense boat steaming upriver, spouting black smoke, and uttering loud whistles.

"*Ahotka!*" shouted the women, pointing at the paddlewheel. It was painted bright red, their favorite color. "Look how it splashes water! Watch how it turns around without anyone touching it!"

The steamboat stopped. The white men on board rowed ashore, distributing vegetable and fruit seeds, and trading colored beads for corn and beans. Meanwhile the white chief walked over to Irataba waiting nearby. "Irataba! I told you I'd remember you!"

Irataba smiled. He recognized Lieutenant Ives, who had been in the surveying party he had guided across the desert.

"And where is Chief Cairook?"

Irataba nodded toward the river. Cairook was standing erect on the center of a raft, a Mohave swimmer at each corner conveying him from the opposite bank. When he arrived, the talk began. Ives explained that he was making an exploration trip in his little stern-wheeler, the *Explorer*, to the Grand Canyon; and he wanted Irataba to go with him as a guide.

It was a frightening prospect to travel on this queer boat to the mysterious Big Canyon where the Hualapais lived. But Irataba courageously assented and persuaded Nah-vah-roo-pa, a boy of sixteen, to accompany him. Blowing her whistle in farewell, the *Explorer* paddled up the great red river.

Irataba sat on deck, pointing out sandbars to be avoided, warning of rapids to be met, and telling the pilot where to anchor for the night. After several days the rapids grew fiercer; the black cliffs on each side towered higher and higher. Then suddenly at the entrance to the forbidding Black Canyon the *Explorer* crashed against a sunken rock.

Thrown full length on deck, Irataba thought the canyon had fallen in. Getting to his knees, he saw that the men near the bow had been pitched overboard; the boiler was thrown out of place; the wheelhouse was torn away. "Take to the skiff before she sinks!" Ives shouted.

The crew made camp on shore, looking sadly at the few beans and corn they had been able to save from the wreckage. "I will go back for food," volunteered Irataba. "But keep guard. I saw a Paiute watching us from a thicket across the river."

Days later he returned, guiding a pack train that had followed the steamer. And now, still remembering the dream which had told him to be afraid of nothing, he led the exploring party into the mysterious depths of the Grand Canyon itself. Here he found some Hualapais to guide the party east toward Fort Defiance. Only then did he turn back home.

Chief Cairook he found in ill humor. All spring the chief kept worrying about these troublesome events. Finally he called a meeting of his five sub-chiefs. "What is happening to our valley?" he asked. "White men come from the east and go to the west. White men come up from the south and go to the north. Here all their trails cross. Our peace is broken. What shall we do being masters of the Colorado?"

When no one answered, he continued. "I say this. Let the white men find a crossing above or below. Not here. When next they come, we shall stop them. The signs are good. Our singers and medicine men, the *hota*, have made magic rings of pebbles on the trail where they will come. And there has been a dream of a great star of fire, with a blazing tail. It is a star of war, a star of blood. What do you say?"

Irataba, friend of the whites, said nothing. But when he heard a low angry murmur, he knew what it meant.

Late that summer a wagon train approached — the first large emigrant train over the thirty-fifth parallel route to California. A rich farmer in Iowa, Leonard John Rose, had heard of the new Great Wagon Road and decided to emigrate to sunny California, where he could breed trotting horses. Outfitting covered wagons, he set out. The large wagon train comprised his own family of seven, his foreman's family, and hired hands to look after a beautiful black stallion, Black Morrill, sixteen trotting horses, and two hundred red Durham cattle. Two months later they reached Albuquerque, New Mexico, where they were joined by eight more families with their stock. Jolting over the Great Wagon Road for two months more, they finally reached the top of the desert mountains and looked down on the Colorado.

Rose took some of the party down to Beale's Crossing to water the stock and to build rafts; the others he left up on the ridge. They had just begun to cook their midday meal when the Mohaves attacked. One man after another fell, pierced with arrows or smashed with clubs.

Into the covered wagons women rushed their children, wrapping them in feather beds for protection. Still the arrows tore through, killing three children. The great stallion, Black Morrill, snorting with rage, lashed out with his forefeet at the Mohaves. The warriors slit his throat, then rushed to the stock milling on the riverbank.

The fight kept up till night. Then Rose and the survivors crept up the ridge to join the rest of the train. Eight of the party had been killed, and thirteen wounded. Of the three hundred head of stock, only eight horses and twelve cattle had been saved. Piling the wounded in one wagon and the children in another, the men and women walking, the emigrants began their torturous journey back to Albuquerque. Stumbling in the dark, listening to the groans of the wounded and the crying children, they saw above them a great star on fire, racing across the dark sky with a blazing tail.

Shocked by news of the massacre, Colonel William Hoffman and fifty dragoons marched from California across the Mohave Desert. The Mohaves attacked, driving them back. Three months later the colonel returned with four companies of infantry, which had been shipped from San Francisco down the Pacific, then up the Gulf and the Colorado to Fort Yuma. From here, with three more companies and four hundred pack animals, they marched upriver to Beale's Crossing. The ground was still littered with pieces of wagons, blackened human bones, and wisps of hair.

More than three hundred Mohave warriors were waiting, but dared not attack such a large army. Colonel Hoffman promptly called a council. A large *ramada* of logs and brush was built. Around it gathered all the armed Mohaves and soldiers. Inside sat Colonel Hoffman and his officers, Cairook and his five chiefs, and the interpreters. Old Cairook wore a little bell around his neck and carried a knife and a pair of rusty scissors in his breechclout. Irataba sat beside him, six feet four inches tall.

The Long Talk began, translated from English to Spanish to Yuman and Mohave, and back again. Colonel Hoffman — "Chief of the Tall White Hat"— coldly stated his terms.

"The Mohaves are never again to molest white men passing through their country. We Americans are going to build a fort here at Beale's Crossing to see they keep the peace. Now let me see the chief who led the attack on the wagon trains."

Cairook was a proud and honest chief. "It was I!"

"So! This then is your punishment. You will give me as hostages three chiefs and the head men of the six leading Mohave families."

Cairook offered himself as a prisoner with the chiefs and head men. The ten men were taken in chains downriver to Fort Yuma. The soldiers remained to establish Fort Mohave on April 28, 1859.

That June news of Cairook's death was brought to Irataba by one of the hostages. He was naked and bleeding, exhausted and starving.

Irataba gave him a gourd of water. "Tell me what happened."

The fugitive's account was simple. The hostages were imprisoned in a small hut exposed to the blazing desert sun. Suffering in the ovenlike heat, one of the chiefs begged the guard to cut his throat. Their misery was so apparent the guards struck off the prisoners' irons and allowed them to walk on the veranda for a breath of air, surrounded by a force armed with muskets and fixed bayonets. Cairook thought of a way to escape, and his brother captives agreed to carry it out. During their airing the next day, the old man seized the guard while the other eight ran for the river. Another guard ran his bayonet through Cairook's body. Still he struggled to reach the river until a musket ball through the head brought him down. Four of the other fugitives were shot and killed. The others escaped.

Brooding over the death of the old chief, Irataba was roused in his *ramada* by a crowd of Mohaves gathered outside. He stepped to the door and waited for their murmur to die down.

"Cairook the chief is dead. We have burned his home and his belongings, as is proper," said a spokesman. "Irataba is chief."

Irataba drew himself up proudly. "It is as I dreamed. I will be your chief."

He governed his people well. Americans up and down the river called him "Chief of the Mohaves, the great tribe of the Colorado Valley, and the finest specimen of unadulterated manhood on this continent." But as more emigrants passed through, and gold-seekers built a settlement named La Paz, the white people began to worry about another Mohave uprising.

"Irataba's influence is keeping the peace along the river and is of more value than a regiment of soldiers," said John Moss, an old-time guide and scout. "Let's take him to Washington and impress upon him the numbers and strength of the white man."

The trip was arranged, and Irataba agreed to go. Now his Great Dream unfolded in full glory. Irataba and Moss traveled to Los Angeles, boarding at San Pedro the steamship *Senator* for San Francisco. Attired in the "full civilized costume" of a black suit and huge white sombrero, Irataba was acclaimed everywhere he went. "He is a big Indian, literally as well as figuratively," reported the *Daily Evening Bulletin* of December 2, 1863, "granitic in appearance as one of the Lower Coast mountains, with a head only less in size to a buffalo's and a lower jaw massive enough to crack nuts or crush quartz."

In January 1864 the two men sailed on the *Orizaba* for New York. Upon their arrival Irataba was dressed in a major general's uniform of fine broadcloth, complete with a yellow sash, and presented with a magnificent gold badge set with colored stones. Suspended from it was a large medal inscribed, "Irataba, Chief of the Mohaves, Arizona Territory." In this regalia he was toured through New York, Philadelphia, and Washington. Crowds heralded his appearance. Government officials and army officers loaded him down with medals, swords, photographs. Finally, heavy with presents and covered with glory, Irataba and Moss sailed for San Francisco and Los Angeles, and were driven by wagon to Beale's Crossing.

The next day Irataba appeared before his people. He was wearing a cocked hat, dressed in his major general's uniform with the yellow sash, decorated with medals, and carrying a long Japanese sword in his belt. He told the Mohaves of all the new and strange things he had seen — the Great Water to the west and to the east, the white-winged ships and snorting steam-wagons, the endless *rancherias* swarming with white people, the great canyons of stone and white iron taller than the walls of the Mohave Canyon, all the riches, glory, and power he had seen.

"So did my Great Dream foretell," he said. "Now it has come true. With my own eyes I have seen it." Somebody in the crowd laughed. Then another shouted, "Irataba, the biggest liar on the Colorado." It was no use. His own people disbelieved him. He had lost his standing in the tribe, and became known as the biggest liar on the Colorado.

Yet he persisted in helping the Mohaves to rout the Chemehuevis. But the Mohave warriors were forced to flee before the Paiutes; and Major General Irataba, entangled in his gaudy uniform, was captured. The Paiutes did not kill him for fear the troops at the fort would avenge his death. Their torture was more cruel. They stripped him of his uniform and sent him back naked and bleeding to his people.

"Chief Irataba! The biggest liar on the Colorado!" the Mohaves taunted when he stumbled weakly home. "Not even the Paiutes would kill him!"

Degraded and shamed, shunning both his own people and the whites, Irataba moved into a little hut. At dawn he rose to greet the sun and hoe his patch of corn, pumpkins, and melons. In the midday heat he returned to his shade and plastered his head and naked body with mud to keep insects away. When the sinking sun grew red enough to stain even redder the red Colorado, he bathed in its muddy flow and sat watching the teal and white herons in the tules. Then it was time to sleep and dream.

Irataba once had dreamed a Great Dream, but it had betrayed him. So he lay and listened to the great river dreaming its own dream, and watched the desert stars grow brighter — the river and the stars that alone had never failed him in any dream of wakefulness or sleep.

As the years passed, his people began to relent of their coldness to him. All along the river more mines were being opened up, more towns being built, more white men passing through their valley, all bringing the new and the strange. Everything Irataba had told them was coming true. Their power was broken. They would never have another chief to replace him, the last independent chief of the Mohaves.

When he died, his people forgave him. They burned his body, his hut, and all his belongings, as was proper. Then they burned their old village as a sign of their greatest respect. They would not touch salt and went without food. So they grieved as people of every race and nation grieve when they do not believe, until it is too late, the dreams and visions of their greatest leaders.

The Warrior Horsemen
of the Great Plains

WEST FROM THE MISSOURI RIVER to the Rocky Mountains and south from Canada to Mexico stretched unbroken the Great Plains — the uncharted sea of grass boundless as the sky above. It was buffalo country — buffalo by the tens of millions, drifting across the plains like shadows of clouds in the sunshine. Indian country too. With Indians of many tribes, all stamped with the same fierce pride of a people free to range the wind-swept space of a timeless land.

These were the fast-riding, buffalo-hunting, warrior horsemen of the Great Plains — centaurs regal in paint and fringed buckskins, with feathered warbonnets hanging to their knees, who epitomize for all the world the wild nobility of the American Indian.

A great peace treaty made at Fort Laramie in 1851 set rough boundaries for the major tribes. All the plains south of the North Platte to the Arkansas River and east of the Rockies through Colorado, Kansas, and Nebraska, were allotted to the Cheyennes and Arapahos. The land south of the Arkansas, in the Panhandle of Texas and Oklahoma, was designated for the Kiowas and Comanches; and that north of the Platte through Wyoming and Montana for the Dakotas or Sioux. Farther north and west ranged the Blackfeet, Crows, and Nez Percés.

On whatever route the covered wagon trains took on their ever-westward march toward the Pacific, they encountered these warrior horsemen swooping down upon them behind chiefs whose names will never be forgotten.

WHITE ANTELOPE SINGS HIS DEATH SONG

White Antelope and Black Kettle, chiefs of the southern Cheyennes, were having trouble holding back their young men from war.

Although the peace treaty of 1851 had allocated them 122,000 square miles of the Great Plains, the Pike's Peak gold rush seven years later had broken the treaty. Thousands of covered wagons with the slogan "Pike's Peak or Bust" painted on their canvas had crawled across the plains. No gold was discovered then at the base of Pike's Peak, yet a new settlement called Denver was growing up a few miles north on Cherry Creek and the Platte. To the south, along the Arkansas, more and more wagon caravans were crawling west toward Santa Fe.

All the plains seemed alive with white men killing off buffalo. The Cheyennes and their close allies, the Arapahos, depended wholly on the immense herds for their subsistence. Buffalo gave them an inexhaustible supply of food — fresh, jerked for winter, or ground with chokecherries. It gave them homes, conical skin lodges big enough to house large families yet easy to move; warm robes for protection against the bleak winds of winter; clothes and moccasins to be beautifully fringed and decorated with colored beads and porcupine quills; sinew for thread and bowstrings. Buffalo gave them a religious symbol.

Yet the alarming decrease in buffalo was not the only cause for the young warriors' unrest. They loved war. They were born to it. Almost every boy was inducted into one of the tribe's seven warrior or soldier societies. From then on he was on the move, and the horse gave him the mobility to race from horizon to horizon. He could ride down on an enemy camp, stampede its horses, and be off with the wind.

There were dogfights and battles, to be sure. But the Cheyennes generally disdained taking scalps. Personal bravery and counting coup brought the highest honor. It was not necessary to kill an enemy to count coup. One had simply to get close enough to touch him with a weapon or the bare hand.

War was a game the Cheyennes played, but a deadly one. The tallest of the Plains Indians, fearless and feared, they earned the name of the Fighting Cheyennes. The most daring of the seven warrior societies was the Dog Soldier Society. It permitted the four bravest of its members to wear the dog rope into battle. One end of this decorated leather band, about ten feet long, the warrior looped around his wrist; the other end was attached to a wooden pin. He would ride into the most furious point of battle and fling himself off his horse. Staking the pin into the ground, he then fought at the end of his short rope until he was killed or the enemy was driven back.

Little wonder that aging Chief White Antelope could not restrain his young men from attacking the hated white men. Sitting in council with all the Cheyenne and Arapaho chiefs, he admitted in his old, tired voice that there was only one answer. They must sign a new treaty giving up all their land in return for a reservation along the Arkansas River in southeastern Colorado. Here, with money from the government, they could buy farm implements and raise crops.

Said Big Mouth quietly, "Do you remember a time when as a Dog Soldier you would bend your head to an enemy, give up your horses, and count coup on a pumpkin?"

White Antelope answered just as quietly, "I remember the time when our great land was empty of white men."

"I will sign," said Black Kettle, wise in years.

All the leading chiefs signed the new treaty in 1861: Little Raven, Storm, Big Mouth for the Arapahos; White Antelope, Black Kettle, Lean Bear for the Cheyennes; and many more. The Dog Soldiers and other small bands refused to sign, calling the treaty a swindle.

Three years later there was still not an Indian living on the reservation marked out for them. A military reservation had been established on the land they were to occupy, making it impossible for them to begin farming. New forts were built along the Arkansas to protect the thousands of wagons traveling the Santa Fe Trail; wagons increased in size to great trains carrying tons of commercial freight, drawn by oxen instead of mules. Professional buffalo hunters were killing off the great herds so fast for hides, leaving the carcasses to rot in the sun, that there was not a buffalo within a hundred miles of the reservation. Facing starvation, the Cheyennes and Arapahos still wandered the plains in search of buffalo; then often rode down on the caravans.

In January 1864 a delegate to Congress wrote the commissioner of Indian affairs of their sad plight, asking that the troops stationed at Fort Lyon on the Arkansas be removed from the reservation to a location between the Indians and the white settlements to the north. His plea was ignored.

Late in June, Governor Evans of the Territory of Colorado issued a proclamation calling for friendly Cheyennes and Arapahos to go to Fort Lyon, and warning that all hostile would be pursued and killed. In an effort to make peace with Governor Evans, Black Kettle and six other chiefs were taken to Denver in September by Major Edward Wynkoop, commanding officer of Fort Lyon, who was sympathetic to the Indians. The Cheyenne chiefs included White Antelope and Black Kettle. Insisting that the two tribes go to Fort Lyon, Evans declined to make a peace treaty. White Antelope and Black Kettle, complying upon their return, moved the Cheyennes to an encampment on Sand Creek about forty miles northeast. Here they were joined by a band of starving Arapahos under Left Hand.

Major Wynkoop at Fort Lyon was severely reprimanded for taking the chiefs to Denver, and accused of being too friendly with the Indians. And early in November he was replaced by Major Scott J. Anthony as commander of the fort. Anthony assured Black Kettle and other peace chiefs that they would be safe at their camp on Sand Creek. This was a false promise. He was urging them to remain there only to keep them within striking distance until he received reinforcements to attack the camp and then move upon a larger village on Smoky Hill, sixty miles farther north.

Reinforcements were on the way. For this was election year, and the Reverend John M. Chivington of Denver, a brawny ex-elder of the Methodist Episcopal Church and a religious fanatic who called himself the "Avenging Angel," was running for office as a delegate to Congress on the statehood bill. In case Colorado was not admitted as a state in the union, he was also running for the office of territorial delegate. To make himself popular, he initiated with Governor Evans the formation of a militia of one-hundred-day volunteers to save Colorado from the depredations of the Cheyennes and Arapahos. He was appointed colonel in command. His four mounted companies of Colorado Volunteers were not soldiers by any stretch of the imagination. Toughs and bullies without discipline, they had been drawn up from the tag-ends of the frontier. Their one desire was to kill Indians on sight.

Chivington arrived at Fort Lyon with his troops on November 28. He immediately threw a cordon of pickets around the post, prohibiting anyone to leave under penalty of death. Then he called a staff meeting of all officers to announce imperiously his intention to attack the Indian camp on Sand Creek. Several of Major Anthony's officers indignantly protested, saying that the chiefs had been promised safety.

The "Avenging Angel" pounded on the table with rage. "Damn any man who sympathizes with Indians! Such men as yourselves had better get out of the service. I have come to kill Indians!"

So that evening of November 28, 1864, the troops left Fort Lyon: Chivington's four mounted companies of some 700 Colorado Volunteers with two twelve-pound Mountain Howitzers, and Major Anthony's command of 125 men and two howitzers. Robert Bent and the noted guide Jim Beckwourth, now an old man of sixty-nine, were forced to serve as guides. The long column of fours rode at cavalry pace — walk, trot, gallop, repeat. Snow covered the sunken buffalo wallows. Tufts of grass stuck up, silvered with frost. All through the night the men rode.

At dawn the column reined up. "The Sandy!" muttered a guide. A wide sandy creek covered with paper ice lay before them. A long line of buffalo-skin lodges, smoke-grey in the dim light, extended along the north bank — about one hundred southern Cheyenne lodges and perhaps twenty more lodges of the Arapahos. Most of the men had gone hunting, leaving only sixty men in the village, half of whom were old or ailing. The lodges were mainly occupied by women and children.

Someone going to the creek for water gave the alarm. The wakened Cheyennes and Arapahos rushed out of their lodges. Hoisting an American flag, Black Kettle shouted to his people to have no fear as they had been promised safety.

Colonel Chivington gave his orders: "Kill and scalp all Indians, big and little! Nits make lice!" The battery of howitzers cut loose, followed by the charge of cavalry. Black Kettle ran to the sand pits for safety, bearing his wife, who was carrying the wounds of nine bullets. Behind him One-Eye, Yellow Wolf, War Bonnet, and other chiefs were cut down. Pursued by the soldiers, women and children fled up the stream bed. A pregnant woman came out of her lodge only to be slashed open with a saber and stamped on by cavalry boots. A group of some thirty terrified women sent out a six-year-old girl with a white rag tied on a stick. The soldiers shot her down, then killed all the women. Everywhere fleeing women and children, holding up their hands for mercy, were killed and scalped.

White Antelope, seventy-five years old, calmly stood before his lodge with folded arms, singing his death song. His voice was no longer tired and shaky. It rang out clear and firm in the frosty morning:

> Nothing lives long,
> Except the earth and the mountains.

The troops cut him down as he sang. One cavalryman scalped him. Another sliced off his nose and ears. A third cut off his testicles — to make a tobacco pouch of his scrotum, the trooper boasted.

The carnage and mutilation of bodies, both men and women,

continued till afternoon. The soldiers then looted the village of all its buffalo robes, trade blankets, and beaded and quilled buckskin clothing; set fire to the lodges; and divided among themselves the horse herd of some 600 ponies.

Chivington reported that he had killed between 400 and 500 people. His report was exaggerated; the number was later determined to be about 30 men and 125 women and children. Chivington then proudly marched back to Denver, where he was given a hero's welcome. Down the street paraded his troops carrying bloody Indian scalps, some of which were displayed in a theater that night. Three children taken prisoners were also exhibited in a carnival.

Sentiment changed when details of the massacre became known. A congressional committee indicted Chivington: "He deliberately planned and executed a foul and dastardly massacre which would have disgraced the veriest savage among those who were the victims of his cruelty."

A military commission then conducted an investigation. General Sherman concluded that the Sand Creek victims had been "tortured and mutilated in a way which would put to shame the savages of interior Africa." Colonel Nelson A. Miles called the massacre "perhaps the foulest and most unjustifiable crime in the annals of America." Although no action was taken against the "Avenging Angel," the commission reported, "No one will be astonished that a war ensued which cost the government $30 million and carried conflagration and death to the border settlements." Over all the Great Plains the flames of war spread, the northern Cheyennes allying themselves with the Sioux.

Black Kettle, still seeking peace, had joined efforts with bands of southern Cheyennes and Arapahos, Comanches and Kiowas. Another peace treaty was signed with these four tribes in 1867 on Medicine Lodge Creek in southern Kansas. All agreed to settle on reservations south of the Arkansas. As they could not be moved until Congress ratified this treaty, Black Kettle with 51 lodges of Cheyennes and Arapahos made camp on the Washita River in Oklahoma.

Here again, on a cold November dawn in 1868, an army detachment suddenly rode upon his village without warning. This time both Black Kettle and his wife were killed with 11 warriors and 92 women and children who were running into the icy river to escape. Only 53 women and children escaped death and were taken captive. More than 800 captured horses were then butchered by the soldiers. The Seventh Cavalry regiment which inflicted this "crushing defeat" on "hostile" Indians was led by General George Armstrong Custer, who claimed his troops had killed 103 warriors. The Cheyennes and Arapahos would not forget him.

SATANTA BLOWS HIS HORN

During the same chill November that Chivington was marching to Sand Creek, the famous scout Kit Carson was marching towards a village of Kiowas and Comanches in the Texas Panhandle. Leaving Fort Bascom in eastern New Mexico, he and his 410 soldiers — cavalry, infantry, and artillery — plodded for three weeks across the desolate Staked Plains.

Carson, now a colonel in the army, sat musing each evening before a fire of buffalo chips, the only fuel. In all his varied experience throughout the Southwest, his present assignment seemed the worst. The Kiowas and Comanches, unlike the tall and proud Cheyennes, were banty-legged little warriors who had been horse thieves and mule traders since the Spanish had introduced horses. Now they were raiding the wagon caravans which set out from Fort Smith, Arkansas.

"This has got to be stopped, of course!" he muttered to himself.

But it would be difficult; the Indians were too well backed by *Comancheros*, unscrupulous Mexicans and Americans. At first they had traded with the Comanches and Kiowas for buffalo robes, saving themselves the trouble of killing and skinning their own animals.

They then increased their profits by returning to New Mexico with herds of horses and mules stolen from Texas settlements. And now they were getting rich by ransoming women and children captured by the Indians during wagon raids, and then selling them as slaves or prostitutes. Carson secretly suspected even civil officials and army officers of helping to finance this nefarious practice. The Indians were kept armed with guns, powder, knives, and liquor by the *Comancheros*.

"Post plenty of pickets around the horse herd!" Carson ordered, getting up stiffly from the dying fire.

Late in November the column reached a deserted ruin of crumbling walls. Adobe Walls had been one of William Bent's outflung trading posts. Nearby, in the wide valley of the Canadian River, rose a Kiowa and Comanche village of 150 lodges. A few miles beyond it, a scout reported, stood a larger village of 500 lodges.

Carson sighed. A few years before, he had suffered a fall from his horse and still felt pains in his chest. But he knew he was in for a fight.

So did Satanta — (White Bear of the Kiowas) — as he sat in his lodge that evening. The head chief of the Kiowas was Dohasan, an aging man who depended on his war chiefs for fighting. One of these was the prominent Satanta. Among his people he was known as a daring warrior; a great orator who spoke four Indian tongues, Spanish, and a little English; and literally a colorful character. For council meetings he painted his body bright red. His lodge was painted red, with streamers of red cloth tied to the protruding poles. And on rare occasions when government whites visited him, he spread a red carpet for them to sit on, and served them from a low table painted red. One of his prized possessions was a French horn he had learned to play.

Even among the Americans, Satanta was known for his trickery and cruelty. Despite his friendly contacts with Indian agents and army representatives, he and his warriors had attacked a stage stop near Fort Lyon in Colorado, killing four men. Then he had raided a settlement near Menard, Texas, killing several residents. A short time before, in answer to a proclamation of Governor Evans, he had brought his band of Kiowas to Fort Larned. No one had warned him that he could not approach the fort as usual. As Satanta walked up to the gate, a guard raised his rifle. Satanta promptly shot him through the arm, then ran off the entire post herd of horses. Stories about him were as exaggerated as his appearance. Undoubtedly some of them must have been true, as this one was.

This evening, as usual, he spread a red carpet in his lodge for his guests. Two women brought in low, red tables on which they set platters of buffalo tongue, venison ribs, Mexican tortillas, and a bottle of whiskey, the gift of a *Comanchero*. All the invited war chiefs came in promptly, sat down on the red carpet in front of the tables, and gorged on the feast in silence. When they were through eating, Satanta opened the bottle of whiskey. The talk began. It was evident from the start that Satanta was assuming the responsibility of the aging chief Dohasan to protect the village from the impending attack of the troops in front of the village.

"This Kit Carson. Of him we know. . . ," began one speaker. Satanta cut him short.

"We attack at sunrise," he said. "Be ready. And listen for this." He tapped the French horn beside him.

Next morning Carson was ready for the attack. He had posted his battery of howitzers on a small knoll. Around it began to circle the mounted warriors in advance of the Kiowas' main force. When they came within range, the battery let loose, tearing a hole in the massed warriors. Then Carson's cavalry swept forward to the bugle's "Charge!" But just before the column reached the front line of Kiowas, there sounded from a French horn the piercing call of "Retreat!" The well-trained cavalrymen wheeled their mounts and dashed back.

There then began a ridiculous and tormentingly confusing musical duet. Carson's bugler would no sooner sound "Charge!" than Satanta's horn would call "Retreat!" The cavalry, dashing back and forth in hopeless confusion, were soon completely demoralized.

Carson now became concerned lest a band of Indians outflank and destroy his wagons in the rear. Calling off the battle, he retreated to the supply train. Behind him came Satanta's warriors, setting fire to the prairie grass. Carson and his cavalry finally reached the detachment guarding the supply wagon. Then the full command drove back the Indians with grape from the howitzers.

Reaching the Indian village, the troops destroyed all its supplies — dried meat, berries, buffalo ribs, everything that could be used. The sun was now setting. To its fiery red flare the troops added another conflagration as they set fire to the lodges.

Carson ended the campaign and marched back to Fort Bascom. He reported simply that he had destroyed a village of 150 lodges, killing sixty Kiowas. The Kiowas claimed only the loss of five men. If this was not a rousing victory for Kit Carson, it at least permitted the safe passage of two wagon trains on their way to New Mexico.

By 1874 professional white buffalo hunters were wiping out the last great herds of the southern plains. During the last four years the hide hunters had killed more than seven million buffalo, taking only the hides and tongues and leaving the great bodies to rot. The slaughter was so devastating that never again would great herds blacken the plains.

The Medicine Lodge Treaty had forbidden buffalo hunters to enter the Texas Panhandle. The army made no effort to stop them, maintaining that extermination of the main food supply of the Indians was the only way to defeat them. The hide hunters preparing for their 1874 hunt began to gather at their headquarters in May. The location was the abandoned Adobe Walls trading post in the Panhandle. New log buildings, a general store, and a saloon stocked with whiskey from Fort Dodge made a comfortable rendezvous.

The Indians made careful preparations to attack the post under the leadership of the half-breed Comanche chief Quanah Parker. The attack began on June 27 and lasted three days. Barricaded inside were twenty-eight men and reputedly one woman. The walls were too stout to break through. Only three of the hide hunters were killed and fifteen Indians. Nine of the Comanche bodies lay too close to the fire of the hunters' guns to be carried away. The warriors returned later to give the bodies proper burial, only to find that their heads had been cut off and mounted on the posts of the corral.

This futile attack ended the resistance of the Kiowas and Comanches. The army rushed in troops to destroy their lodges and all of their food and equipment, and to pursue every band and family. One by one the starving groups straggled in to Fort Sill. On June 2, 1875, Quanah Parker led the last band to surrender.

His dramatic past gave way to an equally colorful future. His mother, Cynthia Ann Parker, born in Texas, had been captured when a child of nine by a Comanche war party. Adopted into the tribe, she quickly embraced Comanche ways. She became the teenage wife of Nacoma, a young warrior, and gave birth in 1847 to Quanah, the Comanche word for "fragrance" or "sweet smelling." After living with the tribe for twenty-five years, she was recaptured by the Texas Rangers and returned to the Parker family. But she was no longer Cynthia Ann Parker. She was Nadua, a Comanche woman with two sons and a daughter out on the plains. When she tried to escape and join them, the Parkers put her under guard. Four years later she starved herself to death.

Quanah adjusted to the white man's ways. He met his mother's uncle, Silas Parker, learned English, and soon became a spokesman for the Comanche tribe. He prospered as a rancher, and a politician, and lived with his many wives in a twelve-room house in Quanah, the town named after him. When he died, he was dressed as a Comanche chief and buried beside his mother, Cynthia Ann, and his sister, Prairie Flower. It is said he left twenty-five children.

Satanta, meanwhile, still continued to resist the flood of incoming settlers. In 1871 he and Big Tree with their warriors attacked a wagon train near Fort Richardson, killed seven men, and mutilated their bodies. Both men were captured, tried, convicted for first-degree murder, and sentenced to death. The governor of Texas was induced to commute their sentences to life imprisonment in the state prison at Huntsville. Two years later they were released on parole on the grounds they had committed an act of war rather than murder. Satanta broke his parole, and was arrested and sent back to the Huntsville prison. Here in 1878 he committed suicide by jumping out of a window in the prison hospital.

In 1963 his remains were moved to Fort Sill, Oklahoma, on the old Kiowa buffalo grounds, and buried again with full military honors.

RED CLOUD WINS HIS WAR

Sparks of war were flying north from Sand Creek to set the plains of the Sioux on fire. A chief named for the reddened sky at his birth now rose quickly to command.

Red Cloud was an Oglala, the largest band of the Sioux Nation. Born at the forks of the Platte River in Nebraska, he was now forty-three years old. He was not a chief by birth, but rose to prominence by his own force of character. He was not by nature a warrior, although he had counted eighty coups, but a statesman and a general. Quiet and dignified, he exemplified the integrity and pride of his people.

The Teton Sioux was a powerful confederation of seven council fires that extended along the upper Missouri from Dakota into Nebraska, Wyoming, and Montana. Their own name for themselves was Dakota or Lakota. The Chippewas of Wisconsin had given them the name Na-du-Wa-Su, meaning "serpents" or "enemies," which the French corrupted into "Sioux."

The main cause of alarm to the Sioux in that bloody year of 1864 was the discovery of gold in Montana. John M. Bozeman, a prospector, promptly blazed a wagon road from the Platte River north through Wyoming to the gold camps around Virginia City. Red Cloud just as promptly captured a small detachment of road builders and held them prisoner for two weeks. To the officials of the newly created Territory of Montana he sent word that the Bozeman Trail cut through the buffalo plains of the Sioux. He would not allow any wagons to pass.

The following year government commissioners at Fort Laramie, using threats of force, insisted on Sioux and Cheyenne permission for wagons to pass through their country. Red Cloud refused: "Is this a peace talk, that you threaten to bring soldiers if we do not agree? Why do you pretend to negotiate for land you intend to take by force? Are we children you can frighten with threats? I say you can force us only to fight for the land the Great Spirit has given us."

Stalking out of the tent with Man-Afraid-of-His-Horses, Red Cloud began to unite the Sioux, Brules, Cheyennes, and Arapahos.

The government moved quickly to establish a line of forts to guard the Bozeman Trail. Colonel Carrington with an army of soldiers and civilian workmen garrisoned Fort Reno with 250 men. He then established Fort Phil Kearny with a garrison of 450 men. While a hundred wagons under heavy guard hauled timber from the Bighorn Mountains to build its log stockade, a group of Cheyenne chiefs came to visit Carrington. Among them were Dull Knife, Two Moons, Black Horse, and Red Arm.

"Take your soldiers back to Fort Reno," they begged. "If you do not, we Cheyennes will have to fight with the Sioux."

Colonel Carrington completed the fort, and in 1866 marched north to establish Fort C. F. Smith on the Bighorn River.

The die was cast. Red Cloud's War began.

In it, new stars appeared among the galaxy of chiefs who were to shine brighter in later years: Sitting Bull, Rain-in-the-Face, Roman Nose, Crazy Horse, a dozen others. Red Cloud, the guiding chief, selected Fort Phil Kearny as his target. He kept it under relentless siege. Not a load of hay, nor a wagon of wood, could be brought in except under a strongly armed guard.

Four mornings before Christmas an armed wagon train left the fort to get wood from the nearby mountains. Pickets on the lookout soon signaled that the train was being attacked. Carrington ordered Colonel W. J. Fetterman to lead seventy-nine cavalrymen to its aid.

"Proceed directly to the train," he instructed. "Keep within sight of the fort. Do not follow the Indians beyond Lodge Trail Ridge."

Fetterman, who had boasted, "Give me eighty men and I'll ride through the whole Sioux Nation," disobeyed orders. Decoyed into ambush by Crazy Horse and a half dozen companions, he took a shortcut over the ridge and out of sight of the fort. Red Cloud's massed warriors then swarmed upon them, killed all eighty men, and butchered their bodies beyond recognition.

The whole nation was shocked. Sherman's telegram to President Grant has been often quoted: "We must act with vindictive earnestness against the Sioux, even to their extermination, men, women and children. Nothing less will reach the root of the cause."

Again that summer a work crew from the fort was sent out with an escort of fifty-one troopers. This time the commanding officer took no chances. He removed the wagon boxes from the running gears, arranging them to form a barricade. Red Cloud attacked as usual. This time, however, the troopers were armed with new breech-loading Springfield rifles and stood off the attack until relief arrived from the fort.

Still another band of Cheyennes attacked a group of soldiers in a hay field outside of Fort C. F. Smith, but was forced to retire.

The Fetterman Massacre and the Wagon Box and Hayfield fights sobered the government commissioners. Another treaty meeting was held at Fort Laramie in 1868. Red Cloud, polite and firm as ever, stated his conditions.

"The Bozeman Trail will be closed," he said. "Every fort will be abandoned. Then only can there be peace."

"We agree," said the commissioners. "Sign the treaty."

"Not until the garrison of all the forts are withdrawn," answered Red Cloud.

It was done. The garrisons of the three forts were removed, and the Cheyennes and Sioux burnt all the forts to the ground. For nine years the Bozeman Trail was closed. Red Cloud was the only Indian chief who had won a war with the United States.

Keeping his word never to fight again, he settled down at the Red Cloud, Nebraska, agency. But his success soured. Younger Indians accused him of selling out to the whites, of living on government handouts, of being a reservation Indian. Red Cloud shrugged off these accusations, and still counseled peace. Later he was moved to the Great Sioux Reservation, where in 1881 the agent V. T. McGillycuddy stripped him of his standing as chief of the Oglalas.

CRAZY HORSE AT THE ROSEBUD

Meanwhile, Red Cloud's son-in-law Crazy Horse had emerged as the superlative war chief of the Sioux. Even to us today, more than a century later, his name evokes more than the knowledge we have of him. An aura of something greater, a strange charisma, must always have clung to him.

In battle he rode naked save for a breechclout, his body painted with white hail spots, and a red lightning streak down one cheek. He carried a pebble behind one ear and wore a red-tailed hawk upon his head. His battle cry was, "It's a good day to die!" But he was never touched by a bullet, arrow, or lance. And he never scalped the enemies he killed.

Crazy Horse had three wives at different times, and one daughter who died of smallpox when still a child. He often spent nights or days wandering away from the village. There are no photographs of him, but many observers report that he was of medium build, light-skinned, and with a narrow face. If people were not a little in awe of him, they must have thought him strange. For the origin of his name, we can take our pick from an assortment of versions.

In 1874 came rumors of gold in the Black Hills, the sacred heart of the Great Sioux Reservation established six years before. A cavalry commander at Fort Abraham Lincoln was dispatched to investigate them. He was General George Armstrong Custer, who, as we remember, had destroyed the sleeping village of Black Kettle's peaceful Cheyennes and Arapahos on the Washita.

Years before, when he was only two months out of West Point, where he was an indifferent student, Custer had become an aide to Brigadier General Philip Kearny. Before the end of the Civil War, Custer himself had been appointed a brigadier. The appointment was only temporary, so designated by the prefix "brevet." At the time of his Black Hills assignment, Custer's official rank was lieutenant colonel. However, it was the social custom to permit an officer to be addressed by the highest rank he had received, and Custer was not the man to refuse any favor that might be given him. So General Custer it was, and is.

Now leading his Seventh Cavalry through the Black Hills, Custer confirmed the presence of gold in French Creek. The news brought hundreds of prospectors, establishing the boom camps of Custer City and Deadwood.

The federal government's failure to buy the Black Hills was followed by an attempt to close the Powder River country in Wyoming. This area had been promised for the Indians' perpetual and exclusive use by the Fort Laramie Treaty. Hence a government order issued in December 1875 for all Indians to report to the Great Sioux Reservation was ignored. The tribes instead began to gather at a central camp on the Rosebud, designated by Sitting Bull.

The leader of the tribes was Sitting Bull, a broad-shouldered, six-foot Hunkpapa Sioux about forty years old, with a big head and nose. As a young man he was a noted warrior. In a fight with a Crow he was shot in his left foot, and he still limped from the wound. He was now better known as a medicine man, a dreamer.

His most famous dream or vision came to him during the United States military campaign against the Sioux. Sitting Bull participated in the most sacred of Sioux ceremonies, the Sun Dance. In preparation for the dance he sat on the ground while an attendant cut fifty small pieces of skin off each of his arms, from wrist to shoulder. The helper then attached the ends of two rawhide thongs dangling from the top of the twenty-foot pine pole mounted in the ceremonial plaza. This was done by gashing Sitting Bull's upper chest and inserting the ends of the thongs. He now began slowly dancing around the pole, drawing the thongs even tighter. Dancing without food or water, staring and praying to the sun. Day and night he danced until the thongs were ripped from his body.

That moment came for Sitting Bull after dancing for two days. At the point of losing consciousness he described through parched lips the vision for which he had prayed.

"I see them," he said. "An army of white soldiers. Falling upside down from the sky. We will kill them all. So it will be."

There was no doubt of the influence and authority he exerted among his people. Government leaders also recognized him as the leader of the gathering tribes.

The War Department meanwhile had ordered General Philip Sheridan to draw up a comprehensive plan to finally end the Indian menace. Three armies would take the field.

General George Crook would march north from Fort Fetterman in eastern Wyoming. Colonel John Gibbon would move east from Fort Ellis in Montana. General Alfred H. Terry would move west from Fort Abraham Lincoln in Dakota Territory. The three prongs would converge at the Little Bighorn, and close like talons upon the gathered Cheyennes, Oglalas, Sans Arcs, Miniconjous, and Hunkpapas.

General Crook left Fort Fetterman in the middle of May and on June 17 ran into Crazy Horse's estimated fifteen hundred warriors in the valley of the Rosebud in Montana, just above the Wyoming line. On the meadow blossoming with wild roses and plums, the two forces joined battle. Crazy Horse's warriors charged at once under his familiar battle cry, "It's a good day to die!" Crook's advance company of Crow and Shoshone scouts held them off until Crook managed to organize his troops.

The fight was said to be a standoff. Crook could not claim a victory, having lost eleven men to Crazy Horse's thirty-six. Only his Crows and Shoshones had saved him from sudden disaster. And he was forced back to his supply post to replenish his provisions. For Crazy Horse it was a bigger victory than he knew. He had prevented Crook from joining Terry and Gibbon at their scheduled rendezvous at the junction of the Yellowstone and Rosebud rivers.

General Terry's army had left Fort Abraham Lincoln on the morning of May 17, 1876. A caravan of men, horses, and wagons two miles long, it moved slowly away. In the sky above, a duplicate caravan kept it company. Elizabeth Custer, wife of the general, noted in her book *Boots and Saddles* that the phenomenon vaguely troubled her. As with Crook's defeat a month later, it was one of the omens accompanying the entire campaign.

Regarding Custer, the "Boy General," with his curly golden locks falling to his shoulders, every adjective in the book for praise or condemnation has been applied to him; and he justified the use of every one. His rise in rank was phenomenal. One factor was his undoubted personal bravery. Another may have been that he was the favorite of General Sherman, who with his inborn violence had blasted a wake of devastation through Georgia to the sea. Hating Indians, he had expressed the opinion that they should all be exterminated. He likely felt a kindred spirit in Custer, who also hated Indians and was bent on exterminating them.

Custer was a man who always functioned only on a physical level, never on the mental or spiritual level. He met every challenge with an instant physical reaction which accounted for his bravery and the attention it drew from his army superiors. He loved dogs, and made pets of all kinds of animals. He was vain and self-centered, fond of dressing in gaudy costumes. It always seemed to many of his associates that he was an actor playing a part — which in fact he was.

In 1874 Custer had been transferred to Dakota to serve in the great Sioux campaign. One suspects from what happened that he expected or at least hoped to lead the entire Fort Abraham Lincoln army at the head of his Seventh Cavalry regiment.

Then the Belknap Scandal broke. Irked by disclosures of fraud and corruption on Indian reservations, a congressional committee was formed to investigate; and Custer was called to testify. Custer knew the corrupt practices. Indian tribes, in return for giving up their lands and moving into reservations, were promised annuities in the form of food, clothing, and trade goods to replace the buffalo which had nourished them. The Indian agent on each reservation was solely responsible for issuing these supplies. What did it matter if he reduced the allotments or issued rotten meat to a bunch of destitute Indians, sold the good beef, and pocketed the difference? Indian agents were getting rich, so the agencies were being sold by government officials to the highest bidder.

Custer was no lover of Indians, those "wild beasts." But in his testimony he implicated Secretary of War William Belknap with other government officials; and he also, directly or indirectly, cast a shadow of suspicion upon Orville Grant, brother of the president himself. In the uproar over this scandal, Belknap resigned his office; and President Grant forbade Custer to participate in the Sioux campaign.

General Terry felt sorry for this dashing, gallant officer and obtained the president's clemency. Obtaining Grant's permission to include Custer in his army, General Terry reinstated him in command of the Seventh Cavalry.

When Elizabeth Custer watched the army and its celestial duplicate leave Fort Abraham Lincoln, it looked formidable enough: a company of Indian scouts, 50 officers and 1,000 enlisted men, a battery of Gatling guns, and Custer's cavalry regiment of 750 men.

Despite having just escaped disgrace by the skin of his teeth, Custer was exuberant. He had brought along his brother Tom, his sickly kid brother Boston, and his teenage nephew Armstrong "Autie" Reed, the younger ones to enjoy watching him conduct this great Indian hunt. Custer also had brought a band of a dozen musicians mounted on white horses. General Terry would not permit them on the battle-field when it was reached, so the musicians were dismounted and left at the Yellowstone supply depot. Custer, however, appropriated the white horses.

BATTLE OF THE LITTLE BIGHORN

In mid-June the armies of Terry and Gibbon met at the junction of the Yellowstone and Rosebud rivers. This area on the border of Wyoming and Montana was a network of rivers fed by the runoff from the high Bighorn Mountains to the south: the Little Bighorn flowing into the Bighorn, and it into the Yellowstone, with the Rosebud and Tongue farther east.

Terry and Gibbon agreed on strategy. Their two forces would follow the Yellowstone west to the Bighorn and go up the Bighorn to the Little Bighorn. Custer and his cavalry would ride south along the Rosebud until they intersected an Indian trail found by Major Marcus Reno. It led toward the Little Bighorn, along which the Indians were said to be encamped. Terry's orders to Custer were explicit. He was not to turn off on the trail and attack the Sioux camp. He was to wait for the main forces moving up the Little Bighorn. Terry and Gibbon still expected Crook to join them, not knowing he had been repulsed by Crazy Horse.

So on the afternoon of June 22, Custer's Seventh Cavalry cantered off. Two long-opposing human spirits were coming to a verge that none could escape.

Custer's troops made good time riding up the Rosebud; he was in a hurry. Just where the Indian camp was, he didn't know; but his Indian scouts assured him it was a big one. About midnight on June 24 he ordered the men to strike camp and resume the march. All that night the sleepless men, many of them mere boys, rode wearily on through the darkness. Early in the morning Custer glimpsed from his high ridge the Indian encampment. It lay below on the west bank of the Little Bighorn — six separate circles of lodges of the Cheyennes, Sans Arcs, Oglalas, Hunkpapas, Blackfeet, and Miniconjous. A later estimate gave fifteen hundred lodges containing between twenty-five hundred and three thousand warriors.

How Custer thought he could attack such a massive concentration with his 675 men is a question answered by many conjectures. One of them is that at the time, the National Democratic Convention was ready to open in St. Louis. What might happen if news of a tremendous Indian victory were received by the delegates while they were selecting presidential nominees? Custer well knew, if he remembered his exciting parade after his Washita victory. But this time the victorious parade of the Seventh would wind through the applauding streets of Washington to the very gates of the Capitol itself.

What did it matter if he disobeyed orders by stopping his march twenty or more miles before the point where he was ordered to meet Gibbon's column? He would attack the Indian village hours before Gibbon arrived, and reap the glory of a single-handed triumph.

He now split his troops. Major Frederick Benteen with three companies would proceed down to the left, looking for Indians. Major Reno with three companies was directed to march directly down the valley of the Little Bighorn and attack the camp from the east. Custer himself with five companies would ride around the end and strike the camp at its lower end. Captain Thomas M. McDougall with one company stayed behind to guard the pack train.

It was early Sunday afternoon, June 25. Thickets of wild plum were white with blossom along the river. A little wind was waving the long prairie grass. Then to the brassy, pitiless sky sounded the silvery notes of a military bugle.

Reno was the first to reach the Indian camp. It suddenly erupted Indians like a swarm of angry bees. Fighting them off, the soldiers managed to cross the river and barricade themselves on top of the high bluffs with bits of baggage, dead horses, anything available. Here, with 52 dead and many wounded, without food and water, they were besieged all afternoon. Far down the valley sounded the faint reports of shots. Presumably Custer was coming with reinforcements. None came. All night and the next day they were pinned down on the bluffs. What had happened to Custer?

The Battle of the Little Bighorn, the Custer Massacre, or Custer's Last Stand had reportedly happened in a half hour. Or was it twenty-nine or thirty-one minutes? Who could time the engulfing of 225 men by waves of angry warriors led by Crazy Horse and Gall, and others who never received the wide acclaim due them: Two Moon, Rain-in-the-Face, Crow King, Big Beaver, Spotted Eagle . . . but where was the master strategist Sitting Bull?

In his book *Shadow Catcher*, Charles Fergus quotes James McLaughlin, at seventy-one "a retired, brain-washed Indian agent of the Bureau of Indian Affairs." He had been the agent at the Standing Rock Reservation where Sitting Bull had been assigned. He had adopted Emma Crow King, daughter of one of Sitting Bull's chiefs. Fergus reports him as saying, "When Reno attacked and the rifle balls started ripping through the tepees, Sitting Bull gathered up his wives and children and lit out for the hills. After the battle they sent out riders and overtook him ten miles from the camp. Later he explained it away by saying that his capture would have meant the loss of his medicine to the Sioux." McLaughlin paused, then burst out, "A coward. A liar! An egotist! A fraud! All the faults of the red man and none of his virtues."

Even though McLaughlin acknowledged that the famous Hunk-papa chief and medicine man was the most influential man among his people, McLaughlin's opinion must be looked at in light of later events.

When the rest of the army arrived, they found that Custer and his 225 men had been killed to the last man. Indian women were still scalping, dismembering and mutilating the bodies, and plundering their uniforms.

The only survivors were a few horses, most notably Comanche, Major Myles Keogh's light bay horse, bristling with arrows. General Terry's men took Comanche back to Fort Abraham Lincoln, where he recovered from his wounds. He was made an honored pensioner of the renewed Seventh Cavalry, and, draped in black, walked at its head during parades.

Sitting Bull said of the battle, "Let no man say this was a massacre. They came to kill us and got killed themselves." General Terry called it "a terrible blunder, a sad and terrible blunder." President Grant regarded the massacre as Custer's own unnecessary sacrifice of his troops.

The bare facts bore Grant out. Custer had disobeyed his written orders, failed to reconnoiter the size and strength of the Indian camp, divided his command in the face of a superior force, and blindly attacked 3,000 massed Indian warriors with 225 sleepless men on jaded mounts.

Yet the Boy General found in death the fame he had sought in life. Overnight he became the image of the heroic pioneer winning the West. Paintings and pictures depicted him standing erect, smoking pistol in hand, in the midst of his fallen comrades. Custer's Last Stand! But after more than a century, the image has faded. As Evan S. Connell writes in his meticulously researched biography *Son of the Morning Star*, "Thus, from a symbol of courage and sacrifice in the winning of the West, Custer's image was gradually altered into a symbol of the arrogance and brutality displayed in the white exploitation." But Custer shouldn't be blamed for what he was, the pawn of invisible forces still working today in American society.

At the Little Bighorn, destiny had given one day of victory to the Plains tribes. It lasted no longer. An expanding nation of forty million white people could not be brought to bay by a handful of starving Indians. One after another, every band of Indians was pursued by troops under Colonel Miles, and herded into the huge Sioux Reservation. Crazy Horse with his band of fifteen hundred Oglalas was among the last to enter in May 1877.

General George Crook, whom he had defeated on the Rosebud three years before, arrested him and took him to Fort Robinson. Widespread opinion held that it was planned to send him under heavy guard to St. Augustine, Florida, where he would be imprisoned for life. Crazy Horse suspected that he was to be imprisoned or killed. He drew his knife. Little Big Man grabbed his arm, and Private William Gentles ran him through with his bayonet.

There is little doubt influential whites, military and civilian, were afraid of Crazy Horse's influence. But more needs to be learned about the rumored plan to imprison him, resulting in his death.

The Little Bighorn's tragic experiences may have affected the lives of Custer's two ranking officers, judging from their similar confused action. Major Reno was generally accused of cowardice for staying on his hilltop instead of going to the rescue of his general. Heated controversy raged about him, driving him into drunken lapses during which he got into several scraps with women. In 1879 a general court martial found him guilty of "conduct unbecoming an officer and a gentleman," and dishonorably discharged him after twenty-five years in the service. He died almost penniless in 1889. Not until 1967, seventy-eight years after his death, did a judge advocate rule that he had been improperly dismissed. His remains were reburied in the Little Bighorn battlefield with full military honors.

Major Benteen also cracked up, to the extent of becoming a "drunken nuisance," and was suspended from duty for a year at half pay. In 1888 he was given a medical discharge and retired, dying soon thereafter. In 1902 his body was exhumed and reburied at Arlington.

The effects of the Battle of the Little Bighorn kept spreading. Still to come were the death of Sitting Bull, the battle at Wounded Knee, and the nation's continued sweep of conquest to the Pacific. But the Little Bighorn was the climax of westward expansion. It sealed the "change of worlds" from Indian America to Euro-America, as Chief Seattle put it in his great oration.

THE AFFAIR AT WOUNDED KNEE

By now all the Sioux and Cheyennes except Sitting Bull were confined to the shrinking Sioux Reservation. He had fled with his followers to Canada, where he remained for four years. Canada would not give him a reservation, and his Hunkpapas had no way to feed and clothe themselves. So small bands, half-starved and in ragged clothing, began crossing the border and surrendering.

Sitting Bull and his last group of two hundred people surrendered in 1881. Sitting Bull gave his Winchester rifle to his eight-year-old son Crow Foot to hand to Major D. A. Brotherford, saying afterward that it was the boy who surrendered, not he. Held as a prisoner of war for two years, Sitting Bull was taken to the Standing Rock agency of the Sioux Reservation. He constantly bickered with agent McLaughlin, earlier mentioned, who distrusted and disliked him. He opposed other Indian leaders who wanted to sell some of their land to the government. "Get a scale and sell our earth by the pound!" he stormed at a council meeting. And he made no bones about his hatred of whites: "I've never met an Indian who didn't hate whites, or a white who didn't hate Indians!" He was obstreperous, quarrelsome, vindictive. And yet his were the only voice and actions that kept alive a spark of hope in his defeated and disheartened people.

Curiously enough, it was the same white people who had enthroned Custer as the nation's hero who also adored the mystical medicine man who had defeated him. Sitting Bull, the most famous Indian in the country, was a celebrity everyone wanted to meet. The flamboyant Buffalo Bill Cody called on him in 1885, and persuaded the Sioux chief to join his Wild West Show for a tour of the country. Buffalo Bill advertised him as the "Slayer of Custer." What a picture he made, dressed in a buckskin shirt with its panels of porcupine quills and colored beads, wearing an eagle feather headdress that fell to his moccasins, his face set in stern expression, his big strong body itself denoting the dignity of his race. This was the Indian as America wanted to see him, and crowds formed everywhere for his photo and autograph.

The tribes on the Great Sioux Reservation had capitulated to government demands, selling some eleven million acres, and splitting up the reservation into five smaller reservations. Agency officials distributed food on ration days, and banned ceremonies that had been observed for generations, including the sacred Sun Dance. Epidemics spread, killing members in every village. The pulse of reservation life was dropping dangerously low.

Then, in 1890, came a message of hope. Kicking Bear brought news of the new messiah, Wovoka, who lived among the Paiutes in Nevada.

"It was on the day the sun was blotted out by darkness the vision came to him," Kicking Bear related in a trembling voice. "A vision of the ghosts of all dead Indians coming to help us return to our old way of life!"

"What about the white people?" asked shrewd old Sitting Bull, a medicine man and visionary himself.

"This said the Great Spirit!" related Kicking Bear. "'I will cover the earth with new soil. Under it will be buried all the whites. Over it will roam herds of buffalo that my red children may hunt and rejoice. Go then, and tell these things to all the people that they may make ready for the coming of the ghosts.'"

Wovoka, like his father before him, was a medicine man who lived in a little tule hut in Mason Valley, Nevada. During an eclipse of the sun in 1889 while he was ill, he entered into a trance. It seemed to him that his soul traveled to the spirit world, where the Great Spirit revealed to him that the Indians would regain their inheritance and come into the fullness of their own being. Wovoka claimed no supernatural powers. His vision was one of spiritual redemption. But it spread like wildfire beyond the Rockies, bringing hope to a defeated, frightened people decimated by war, disease, confinement, and starvation. And as the story spread, it changed. Not in the spirit world would Wovoka's prophecy come true, but here on earth.

So now a new religion, the Ghost Dance, was taking hold of the Sioux. On all the reservations Ghost Dances were being held to welcome the coming of the ghosts. The dances were simple enough — throngs of people chanting ritual songs and dancing until they fell exhausted — but keyed to such frenzy that white people readily interpreted them as war dances in preparation for another uprising.

Sitting Bull applied to his agent for a pass to attend one of these dances. McLaughlin, with whom he had carried on a constant feud, ordered his arrest, saying he was either encouraging the ghost dancers or intending to flee. Forty-three Indian policemen under his direction surrounded Sitting Bull's cabin on the morning of December 15, 1890. There are several versions of what happened. Apparently Bull Head, one of McLaughlin's policemen, approached Sitting Bull with a warrant for his arrest. When the big chief angrily protested, Bull Head shot him in the thigh; and Sergeant Red Tomahawk shot him in the head. In the tumult, six policemen and eight of Sitting Bull's followers, including his young son Crow Foot, were killed.

The death of the quarrelsome medicine man Sitting Bull and that of the peaceful war chief Crazy Horse, the two great leaders of the Sioux at the Little Bighorn, offer an interesting parallel.

News of the great medicine man's death spread terror among his people. Bands of confused Sioux milled about on snowy plains, most of them heading for protection on the Pine Ridge Reservation. One of them was a band of 350 people under Chief Big Foot, who was ill with pneumonia. On the afternoon of December 28 they were surrounded by four troops of Custer's renewed Seventh Cavalry under the command of Major Whiteside, and escorted to the base military camp on Wounded Knee Creek. More troops of the Seventh Cavalry arrived, the complete regiment being under Colonel James W. Forsyth. The prisoners — 120 men and 230 women and children — were allowed to set up lodges and tents.

The next morning Colonel Forsyth ordered all Indians to gather outside their lodges and to give up their weapons. Big Foot was brought out to sit in the center, hemorrhaging on his blanket. Around them were posted some 500 cavalrymen on their horses. Behind them four Hotchkiss guns were mounted on a slight rise above the plain and trained on the encampment.

The Indians as ordered laid down on the ground their few guns, knives, and axes. To make sure no guns were being withheld, troopers searched the lodges and made the men remove their blankets. One young warrior raised a rifle above his head in protest against giving up his weapon. A soldier grabbed at it. Somehow the rifle went off. And then it happened, that morning only four days after Christmas.

The revengeful Seventh Cavalry troopers charged in. From the slope the four Hotchkiss guns hurled two-pound shells at the rate of fifty a minute into the encampment. Without arms, the few Indian warriors fought back with lodge stakes, cooking utensils, and their bare hands. No one was spared. Big Foot was riddled with lead. Blankets drawn over their heads, defenseless women were shot while crouching in the snow. Screaming children were run through with bayonets. A few women running over the snowy plain were pursued three miles before they were caught and killed.

When the massacre was over, it was found that more than half of the 250 Indians had been killed, and only 25 troopers, while 23 troopers were awarded Medals of Honor. That night there was a severe blizzard, and the bodies of the dead Indians were left where they fell. Not until New Year's Day could the bodies be dug out from the snow. The photograph of Big Foot's body frozen into a stiff, grotesque position is the most heartbreaking picture of the era.

Such was the tragic affair that our American history textbooks call the "Battle" of Wounded Knee. The defense of the Great Plains by the warrior horsemen, which had begun with the massacre at Sand Creek in 1864 and ended with the massacre at Wounded Knee in 1890, was over. The bow was broken. The last arrow had been spent.

Chief Joseph

YOUNG JOSEPH, FIFTEEN YEARS OLD, had never seen anything like it nor would he ever again — this great show put on by five thousand Indians for one hundred white men. His heart swelled with pride as he sat with his younger brother Alokut beside their father, the chief Old Joseph.

All the great valley of Walla Walla seemed to be one vast encampment of Nez Percé, Cayuse, Yakima, and Klikitat skin lodges. For hours the warriors had been painting their own horses' bodies with yellow, white, and red paint; putting on their warbonnets, plumes, and beads. Now at a signal, they came charging in a solid phalanx toward Joseph and the white men. The earth shook with the thunder of hooves. The air trembled with war cries. The bright May sunlight glinted on their lances, shields, knives, and guns. Then, just as Young Joseph thought he would be run down, the horsemen pulled up, wheeled, and circled for another splendid charge. How wonderful it was! How proud he was of his own Nez Percé, the largest and strongest tribe there!

A few days later his father and the other chiefs settled down to council with Governor Stevens of the Territory of Washington and his one hundred white men. There was nothing for Young Joseph to do but wander around the encampment admiring the great herds of blue Appaloosa horses with black-spotted rumps which were the joy of his people.

When the great peace council was over and they were riding home, he asked his father what the council had been about.

"We have just concluded what you will remember as the Walla Walla Treaty of 1855," said Old Joseph sourly. "By it we Nez Percés have given up some of our hunting ground and accepted a reservation. The government promises to keep out all white settlers, and will give us schools and smithies and such things. I don't like it. But it will prevent war between us and the white men coming every year."

"Will we have to move from our home?" asked Young Joseph.

"Give up our Wallowa Valley? Never!" snorted Old Joseph.

He had reason to feel secure. The Nez Percé was the strongest and largest tribe in the Northwest. They lived in the country around the big bend of the Columbia River in Washington, Oregon, and Idaho. The early French trappers had given them the name of Nez Percés, "Pierced Noses," because they pierced their noses for shell ornaments. Joseph's own band of Nez Percés occupied the immense Wallowa Valley, three times the size of Rhode Island, in northeastern Oregon. French trappers, missionaries, and Lewis and Clark, the American explorers, all regarded them as friendly, peaceful, devoutly religious Indians. Even Old Joseph gave up his name of Tu-eka-kas and embraced Christianity, and had his son baptized and given the same Christian name.

Young Joseph, however, grew up as a true Nez Percé. At the age of puberty he observed the lonely sacred vigil prescribed by the medicine man, and received a dream. Although he never told the dream in its entirety, according to tradition, he was then given the ceremonial name of Hin-mut-too-yan-lat-kekht, "Thunder Rolling in the Mountains." And so he grew up loving the land as his Mother, in the immense Wallowa Valley of his ancestors.

But things were happening fast. American settlers were pouring in over the Oregon Trail. The Territory of Oregon was established, and from it was created the Territory of Washington. More and more white settlers kept rolling in, and so Old Joseph had signed the 1855 treaty to avoid bloodshed.

As the land-hungry settlers kept coming, Old Joseph pleaded with the Indian agent, "Why don't you keep them out?"

"Humph!" he retorted. "To attempt to restrain them would be, to my mind, like attempting to restrain the whirlwind!"

So in 1863 another great peace council was called at Fort Lapwai, Idaho. Again Young Joseph and his brother Alokut went with their father and some two thousand Nez Percés. Joseph was now twenty-three years old, standing six feet two inches tall, a handsome young man with an alert mind. During the long conference he met the young daughter of Chief Whisk-tasket, and fell in love with her at once. Following the prescribed ritual, they were married and within two years had a daughter, Sarah Moses.

His courtship did not deafen him to the talks that went on day after day. "It is impossible to keep out the land seekers, as you well know," the white Indian commissioners kept saying. "So let us adjust the boundaries of your land." The adjustment they proposed reduced Nez Percé land from ten thousand to twelve hundred square miles, and took away their Wallowa Valley.

Old Joseph was aghast. "The government hasn't kept the treaty of 1855 when it stole part of our land! Where are the annuities, the schools, everything else it promised? And now you want to take most all the land left us!"

But Chief Lawyer, and other chiefs, tempted by promises of large annuities, signed the treaty.

Old Joseph rode home to Wallowa Valley in a rage. He tore up his copy of the treaty and his New Testament. Then he planted poles around the valley. "Inside is the home of my people," he declared. "The white men may take the land outside. Inside this boundary all our people were born. It circles around the graves of our fathers, and we will never give up these graves to any man."

Eight years later when he lay dying, he called to Young Joseph. "When I am gone, think of your country," he counseled. "You are the chief of these people. They look to you to guide them. A few more years and the whites will be all around you. They have their eyes on this land. My son, never forget my dying words. Never sell the bones of your father and mother."

So Young Joseph at the age of thirty-one became Chief Joseph of the Wallowa Nez Percés. His responsibility required all of his tact and firmness.

Homesteaders kept usurping land in the Wallowa, but Joseph restrained his people from fighting them. To government officials he explained with dignity and determination that, according to Indian custom, those bands which did not sign a treaty were not bound to it. The whites, on the contrary, insisted that Chief Lawyer's signature on the treaty bound all bands.

"Neither Lawyer nor any other chief had authority to sell this land," Joseph answered. "It has always belonged to my people. It came unclouded to them from our fathers, and we will defend this land as long as a drop of Indian blood warms the hearts of men."

As a result of this firm stand, President Grant issued in 1873 an executive order withdrawing Wallowa Valley from settlement as public domain. Two years later the president in a new proclamation threw it open again. Patiently Joseph counseled peace, inducing his people to move their lodges away from the camps of the settlers who kept trying to provoke war. Then in 1877 General Oliver O. Howard arrived from Fort Lapwai, Idaho, with news that the Nez Percés were to be moved to a reservation at Lapwai. Joseph, Chief Tuhulkutsut, and Smohalla, the religious leader, protested.

"The land is our mother," said Joseph. "She should not be disturbed by hoe or plow. We want only to subsist on what she freely gives us."

Smohalla spoke: "You ask me to plow the ground! Shall I take a knife and tear my mother's bosom? Then when I die she will not take me to her bosom to rest.

"You ask me to dig for stone! Shall I dig under her skin for her bones? Then when I die I cannot enter her body to be born again.

"You ask me to cut grass and make hay and sell it, to be rich like white men! But how dare I cut off my mother's hair?"

Repeated Tuhulkutsut, "The earth is part of my body. I belong to the land out of which I came. The earth is my mother."

General Howard slapped his hand down on the table: "Twenty times over repeat that the earth is your mother! . . . Let us hear it no more, but come to business at once!"

That business was simple. He gave the Nez Percés thirty days to move to the Lapwai Reservation before bringing in his troops.

Joseph returned home; sadly he gave his people orders to strike their lodges and make ready to leave. "I said in my heart that rather than have war, I would give up my country. I would give up my father's grave. I would give up anything rather than have the blood of white men upon the hands of my people."

So early in the summer, some five hundred Nez Percé men, women, and children, with their two thousand horses, lodges, and belongings, began the trek from their ancestral homeland. Eleven days before their time was up, the bands under Chief Joseph, Looking Glass, White Bird, and Tuhulkutsut reached Rocky Canyon. Here a dreadful thing happened. Three young warriors, homesick and enraged, went on a rampage and murdered eighteen settlers. General Howard rushed troops to the area. The war that Joseph had tried so long to avoid had begun.

A few days later White Bird Canyon troops and Indians met in their first battle. The Indians completely outmaneuvered and outshot the soldiers, killing thirty-three with a loss of only four warriors. Joseph issued strict orders: "Leave the bodies of the soldiers untouched. Do not take scalps!"

General Howard immediately ordered to the field a column of cavalry, infantry, and artillery — some four hundred men. Chief Joseph retreated. He had begun that masterly march which was to be compared to Xenophon's March of Ten Thousand, and which was to earn him the name of the "Red Napoleon of the West."

Early in July the two forces met in battle again at Clearwater

River. General Howard, who had helped to plan the union strategy at Gettysburg, was amazed at the clever tactics employed, and he assumed that Chief Joseph was a military genius. Joseph, however, was not a war chief. He depended upon White Bird, Looking Glass, Yellow Bull, Tuhulkutsut, and his brother, Alokut, whom he called He Who Led the Young Men. But Joseph bore sole responsibility for picking the route, managing five hundred people with two thousand horses, finding provisions, and looking after the women, children, aged, ill, and wounded. It was his decision after the battle to abandon eighty tepees, flour, jerked beef, and buffalo robes and to march northeast toward Canada.

The way led over the steep Lolo Trail in the Bitterroot Mountains, littered with rock slides and fallen timber. He now sent messengers to ask the Crows for permission to pass through their country in Montana. At the summit he learned from scouts that the whole countryside was alarmed and the settlers at Missoula were arming against him, so he turned south to Big Hole Valley. In its rich meadow he pitched ninety tepees and gave his people and horses a rest.

Then disaster struck. Fresh troops under Colonel John Gibbon, in a surprise attack, routed the warriors and captured the village. Joseph heard Looking Glass's voice shouting above the turmoil. He was calling out the names of the three young men who had started the war by murdering the settlers: "This is battle! Now is the time to show your courage and fight. I would rather see you killed than the rest, for you commenced the war. Now fight!"

All three were killed, with nineteen other warriors and seventy women and children, including Joseph's two wives; but their desperate charge won back the village. Still there was no rest, for General Howard's column came up. Joseph moved on, coming back into Idaho. By late August the weary refugees were at the boundary of Yellowstone National Park, traveling north to Canada. Behind him General Howard was having just as rough traveling. He abandoned his supply wagons and continued with pack horses.

Joseph was now in desperate straits. Howard's army was close behind him. Colonel Samuel D. Sturgis with another cavalry column was coming to flank him from the east. And the Crows had allied themselves with the white army. In a brilliant maneuver, Joseph outwitted and escaped Sturgis; but in a running battle extending for 150 miles through Canyon Creek he lost 21 men and was forced to abandon 500 jaded ponies.

By late September he had reached Cow Island on the Missouri River. Short of food, he managed to capture 50 tons of supplies just unloaded from a steamer. He then hurried on to the north slope of the Bear Paw Mountains and stopped to give his weary people and gaunt horses a rest. They needed it; the sight of them broke his heart. In four months he had led them across four states: Washington, Oregon, Idaho, and Montana; twice across the Continental Divide; through a portion of Yellowstone National Park; and across the Missouri River — a journey of some 1,700 miles, half of it through the rugged Rockies. But Canada, where Sitting Bull's band of Sioux was encamped, was only 30 miles away. Here in the land of Redcoats he would be safe.

This delay, necessary as it was, proved fatal. For General Howard had sent an order by boat down the Yellowstone River for General Nelson A. Miles at Fort Keogh, near Miles City, to intercept Chief Joseph before he reached Canada. Miles, with a force of 375 cavalrymen, struck Joseph's camp from the southeast with a surprise cavalry charge on September 30. The fresh, mounted Bluecoats, sabers flashing and guns cracking, might well have struck terror into the hearts of the weary Nez Percés. But as one saddle after another was emptied of its cavalry riders, the soldiers met the savage ferocity of a homeless people fighting for their lives — crackshot warriors and superb horsemen who in dazzling countercharges knifed through their ragged lines. By day's end when the cavalry withdrew, their casualties were heavy; 53 men out of 115 in one battalion had been killed, and half the force of another battalion.

Chief Joseph was desolate. His horse had been shot out from under him; his clothes were riddled with bullets. His brother Alokut, Looking Glass, Tuhulkutsut, and Pile of Clouds had been killed. How many other warriors and women had been killed he did not know, nor was there time to find out. A heavy snow was falling. By midnight, with the rise of a strong wind, a blizzard was adding to the misery of this unprotected people.

In despair he sent six messengers to ask Sitting Bull to come to his aid. No answer came back. The messengers, he found out later, had been murdered by Assinboines for their guns. Also, shrewd Sitting Bull, hearing of the battle, had retreated forty miles farther north. To add to Joseph's plight, White Bird with 104 people broke through the soldiers' picket lines and escaped to join Sitting Bull. With them went Joseph's daughter, Sarah, leaving him with a baby girl only five months old.

"We could have escaped from Bear Paw Mountains," Joseph said later, "if we had left our wounded, old women, and children behind. We were unwilling to do this. We had never heard of a wounded Indian recovering while in the hands of white men."

For a few days more the band continued to freeze and fight, living in burrows and eating the flesh of dead horses. Meanwhile, Miles was in front of them, Howard behind, and Sturgis was following with his troops. There was no escape. Wearily, Joseph agreed to talk over terms of his surrender with General Miles.

The terms were brief. General Miles promised to spare the lives of his people, and to send them to their reservation.

On the afternoon of October 5, Joseph rode, with five men walking beside his horse, to the hill on which General Miles and his officers were waiting. The sinking red sun lit up his buckskin leggings, his blanket filled with bullet holes, and his bowed head with the scalp lock tied with otter fur. He swung off his horse, leaving it to his companions to hold, and walked alone up to the general. Opening his blanket, he offered his rifle to General Miles. Then raising his right arm to point at the still reddening sun, he delivered his immortal speech of surrender. When he finished, he drew his blanket over his bowed head in a gesture of humiliation, and walked to the army tent prepared for him.

CHIEF JOSEPH'S SPEECH OF SURRENDER

Recorded by Lieutenant C. E. S. Wood,
aide-de-camp of General Howard.

Tell General Howard I know his heart. What he told me before I have in my heart. I am tired of fighting. Our chiefs are killed. Looking Glass is dead. Tuhulkutsut is dead. The old men are all dead. He Who Led the Young Men is dead. It is cold and we have no blankets. The little children are freezing to death. My people, some of them, have run away to the hills, and have no blankets, no food. No one knows where they are, perhaps freezing to death. I want to have time to look for my children and see how many I can find. Maybe I shall find them among the dead.

Hear me, my chiefs! I am tired. My heart is sick and sad. From where the sun now stands, I will fight no more forever.

Behind Joseph his defeated people straggled in across the snowy plain — 87 warriors, 40 of whom were wounded; 184 women and 147 children, sick, freezing, and half-starved; and 1,100 gaunt horses.

In their 1,700-mile march through hostile country, and without a base of supplies, their 350 warriors had held off 2,000 army troops, fought 11 engagements, and inflicted 266 casualties.

Said General William Tecumseh Sherman:

> The Indians throughout displayed a courage and skill that elicited universal praise; they abstained from scalping, let captive women go free, and did not commit indiscriminate murder of peaceful families, which is usual, and fought with almost scientific skill.

General Miles wrote to the secretary of war:

> As these people have been hitherto loyal to the government and friends of the white race from the time their country was first explored, and in their skilful campaign they have spared hundreds of lives and thousands of dollars worth of property that they might have destroyed, and as they have, in my personal opinion, been grossly wronged in years past. . . . I have the honor to recommend that ample provision be made for their civilization.

Nevertheless, the secretary of war, on the advice of General Sherman, refused to honor Miles's promise to Chief Joseph. The Nez Percé prisoners were sent to Fort Leavenworth, Kansas, in the malarial bottomlands of the Missouri River, where many of them died. The surviving 268 Nez Percés in 1885 were then transferred to Indian Territory, where still more died. Those remaining were finally returned to the Northwest: part of them to the Lapwai Reservation in Idaho, Chief Joseph and the rest to the Colville Reservation near Nespelem, Washington. Here, according to his physician, Chief Joseph died in 1904 of a broken heart, pining for the land and the graves of his fathers.

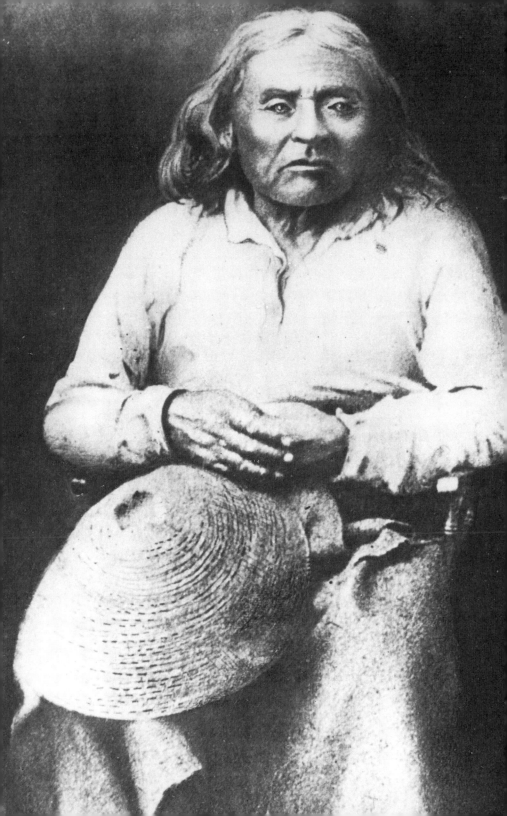

Chief Seattle

CHIEF SEATTLE OF THE DUWAMISH TRIBE, for whom the city of Seattle, Washington, is named, had been friendly to the white man. But the flood of settlers following the California gold rush of 1849 demanded their land. Chief Seattle, upon agreeing to sign the Port Elliot Treaty, by which the Duwamish tribe gave up its lands in the Puget Sound region and accepted confinement on a reservation, made the following oration before Isaac Stephens, governor of the Territory of Washington, in 1854.

The speech was delivered in the Salish tongue. Its only known translation, according to historian David Buerge, was made by a Dr. Henry Smith, who published it in 1887. Other versions, some obviously spurious, have been made. The Smith translation, given here, is considered to be the closest reflection of the actual words spoken by Chief Seattle.

Chief Seattle was a great speaker and skilled diplomat. Born in 1786, he died in 1866 at the age of eighty, one year after the city named for him passed a law making it illegal for Indians to live in Seattle. Here is the Smith translation of the greatest of all Indian orations.

Yonder sky that has wept tears of compassion on our fathers for centuries untold, and which to us appears changeless and eternal, may change. Today is fair. Tomorrow it may be overcast with clouds. My words are like the stars that never change. Whatever Seattle says, the great chief at Washington can rely upon with as much certainty as he can upon the return of the sun or the seasons.

The White Chief says that the Big Chief in Washington sends

greetings of friendship and goodwill. This is kind of him, for we know he has little need of friendship in return. His people are many, like the grass that covers the vast prairies. My people are few, and resemble the scattering trees of a storm-swept plain. . . .

Your God is not our God. . . . We are two distinct races with separate origins and separate destinies. There is little in common between us. To us the ashes of our ancestors are sacred and their resting place is hallowed ground. You wander far from the graves of your ancestors and seemingly without regret. Your religion was written on tablets of stone by the iron finger of your God so that you could not forget it. The Red Man could never comprehend nor remember it. Our religion is the traditions of our ancestors — the dreams of our old men given them in the solemn hours of the night by the Great Spirit, and the visions of our sachems; and it is written in the hearts of our people.

Your dead cease to love you and the land of their nativity as soon as they pass the portals of the tomb and wander way beyond the stars. They are soon forgotten and never return. Our dead never forget the beautiful world that gave them being. . . .

Day and night cannot dwell together. The Red Man has ever fled the approach of the White Man, as the morning mist flees before the morning sun. However, your proposition seems fair and I think that my people will accept it and will retire to the reservation you offer them. Then we will dwell apart in peace.

It matters little where we pass the remnants of our days. They will not be many. A few more moons, a few more winters — and not one of the descendants of the mighty hosts that once moved over this broad land or lived in happy homes, protected by the Great Spirit, will remain to mourn over the graves of a people once more powerful and hopeful than yours. But why should I mourn at the untimely fate of my people? Tribe follows tribe, and nation follows nation, like the waves of the sea. It is the order of nature, and regret is useless. Your time of decay may be distant, but it will surely come; for even the

White Man, whose God walked and talked with him as friend with friend, cannot be exempt from the common destiny. . . .

Every part of this soil is sacred in the estimation of my people. Every hillside, every valley, every plain and grove, has been hallowed by some sad or happy event in days long vanished. Even the rocks which seem to be dumb and dead as they swelter in the sun along the silent shore, thrill with memories of stirring events connected with my people. The very dust upon which you now stand responds more lovingly to their footsteps than to yours, because it is rich with the blood of our ancestors and our bare feet are conscious of the sympathetic touch. Even the little children who lived here and rejoiced for a brief season, will love these somber solitudes and at eventide greet shadowy returning spirits.

When the last Red Man shall have perished, and the memory of my tribe shall have become a myth among the White Men, these shores will swarm with the invisible dead of my tribe. And when your children's children think themselves alone in the field, the store, the shop, upon the highway, or in the silence of the pathless woods, they will not be alone.

At night when the streets of your cities and villages are silent, and you think them deserted, they will throng with the returning hosts that once filled and still love this beautiful land. The White Man will never be alone.

Let him be just and deal kindly with my people, for the dead are not powerless. Dead, did I say? There is no death, only a change of worlds.

Plate Credits

Prayer to the Mystery, 1908, by Edward Curtis, vol. 3, no. 91 of *The North American Indian*, courtesy of the Museum of Indian Arts and Culture/Laboratory of Anthropology, Santa Fe, N. M., cover.

The Great Tree of Peace. Lithograph of painting by Oren Lyons, courtesy of Onondaga Savings Bank, Syracuse, N. Y., p. 6.

Powhatan, or Wah-un-so-na-cook. From original drawing, artist unknown; illustration from *Lives of Famous Indian Chiefs* by Norman B. Wood (Aurora, Ill.: American Indian Historical Publishing Co., 1906), p.15.

Massasoit and the Pilgrim Fathers. Bas relief on the national monument at Plymouth, Massachusetts, courtesy of FPG International Corp., New York, N.Y., p.24.

Pontiac. From original painting, artist unknown; illustration from *Lives of Famous Indian Chiefs*, by Norman B. Wood (Aurora , Ill.: American Indian Historical Publishing Co., 1906), p. 34.

Thayendanegea, or Joseph Brant. From portrait by George Catlin after Ezra Ames, 1806; illustration from *Life of Joseph Brant (Thayendanegea)*, vol. 2, by William L. Stone (Albany, N.Y.: J. Munsell, 1865), p.44.

Red Jacket. Lithograph after painting by C. B. King from *lives of Famous Indian Chiefs*, by Norman B. Wood (Aurora Ill.: American Indian Historical Publishing Co., 1906), p.52.

Tecumseh. Painting, artist unknown, courtesy of Field Museum of Natural History, Chicago, Ill. (Neg. no. A93851.1), p.58.

Black Hawk. After George Catlin in *Letters and Notes on the Manners, Customs, and Conditions of the North American Indians*, vol. 2, 4th ed. (London: David Bogue, 1844), courtesy of Smithsonian Institution, Washington, D.C. (Neg. no. 658-c), p.68.

Sequoyah. Painting by Robert Lindneux, courtesy of Woolaroc Museum, Bartlesville, Okla. (Neg. no. GRA-174), p.78.

Osceola. Detail from lithograph, artist unknown, courtesy of the Bettman Archive, New York, N. Y., p.90.

Mangas Coloradas, Drawing by Clarence Batchelor, courtesy of Museum of New

Mexico, Santa Fe, N. M. (Neg. no. 14220), p.100.

Manuelito. Photograph by Charles M. Bell, 1874, courtesy of Museum of New Mexico, Santa Fe, N.M. (Neg. no. 15949), p.112.

Irataba. Mohave Chief Irataba, detail from lithograph by Baldwin Mollhauser, courtesy of San Diego Museum of Man, San Diego, Calif., p.124.

Sitting Bull. Photograph by David F. Barry, courtesy of Denver Public Library Western History Department, Denver, Colo. (Neg. no. 10309), p.136.

Chief Joseph. Photograph by Edward H. Latham, ca. 1903, courtesy of Special Collections Division, University of Washington Libraries, Seattle, Wash. (Neg. no. NA 606), p.168.

Chief Seattle. Detail from photograph, photographer unknown, courtesy of Washington State Historical Society, Tacoma, Wash., p. 180.

Bibliography

Armstrong, Virginia I., ed. *I Have Spoken: American History through the Voices of the Indians*. Chicago: Swallow Press, 1971.

Ball, Eve. *In the Days of Victorio: Recollections of a Warm Springs Apache*. Tucson: University of Arizona Press, 1970.

Brandon, William. *The American Heritage Book of Indians*. Edited by Alvin M. Josephy, Jr. New York: American Heritage Publishing Co., 1961.

Brown, Dee. *Bury My Heart at Wounded Knee*. New York: Holt, Rinehart and Winston, 1970.

Bryan, William Jennings, ed. *The World's Famous Orations*. Vol. 8. New York: Funk and Wagnalls, 1906.

Capps, Benjamin. *The Great Chiefs*. Alexandria, Va.: Time-Life Books, 1975.

Collier, John. *The Indians of the Americas*. New York: W.W. Norton and Co., 1947.

Comfort, Will L. *Apache*. New York: E. P. Dutton, 1931.

Connell, Evan S. *Son of the Morning Star: Custer and the Little Bighorn*. Berkeley, Calif.: North Point Press, 1984.

Crosby, Alexander L., ed. *Steamboat Up the Colorado*. Boston: Little, Brown and Co., 1965.

Driver, Harold E. *Indians of North America*. Chicago: University of Chicago Press, 1969.

Edmunds, R. David, ed. *American Indian Leaders: Studies in Diversity*. Lincoln: University of Nebraska Press, 1980.

Foreman, Grant. *Indian Removal*. Norman: University of Oklahoma Press, 1932.

———. *Sequoyah*. Norman: University of Oklahoma Press, 1959.

Grinnell, George Bird. *The Cheyenne Indians: Their History and Ways of Life*. 2 vols. New Haven, Conn.: Yale University Press, 1923.

———. *The Fighting Cheyennes*. Norman: University of Oklahoma Press, 1956.

Hewitt, J. N. B. *A Constitutional League of Peace in the Stone Age*. Washington, D.C.: Smithsonian Institution, 1918.

Hoebel, E. Adamson. *The Cheyennes*. Toronto: Holt, Rinehart and Winston of Canada, 1960.

Howard, Helen Addison, and Daniel L. McGrath. *War Chief Joseph*. Lincoln: University of Nebraska Press, 1941.

Jackson, Donald, ed. *Black Hawk: An Autobiography*. Urbana: University of Illinois Press, 1964.

Johnston, Charles H. L. *Famous Indian Chiefs*. Boston: C. L. Page and Co., 1938.

Jones, Louis Thomas, Ph. D. *Aboriginal American Oratory*. Los Angeles: Southwest Museum, 1965.

Josephy, Alvin M., Jr., ed. *The Nez Percé Indians and the Opening of the Northwest*. New Haven, Conn.: Yale University Press, 1965.

Kelsay, Isabel Thompson. *Joseph Brant, 1743–1807: Man of Two Worlds*. Syracuse, N. Y.: Syracuse University Press, 1984.

La Farge, Oliver. *A Pictorial History of the American Indian*. New York: Crown Publishers, 1956.

Lavender, David. *Bent's Fort*. New York: Doubleday and Co., 1954.

Lyons, Oren R., and John C. Mohawk, eds. *Exiled in the Land of the Free: Democracy, Indian Nations, and the U. S. Constitution*. Santa Fe, N. M.: Clear Light Publishers, 1992.

McNichols, Charles L. *Crazy Weather*. New York: Macmillan Publishing Co., 1943.

McReynolds, Edwin C. *The Seminoles*. Norman: University of Oklahoma Press, 1957.

Morgan, Lewis Henry. *League of the Ho-De-No-Sau-Nee or Iroquois*. New York: Dodd, Mead and Co., 1904.

Nelson, Bruce. *Land of the Dakotas*. Lincoln: University of Nebraska Press, 1946.

Parkman, Francis. *The Conspiracy of Pontiac*. 2 vols. Boston: Little, Brown and Co., 1908.

Powell, Peter J. *People of the Sacred Mountain*. 2 vols. San Francisco: Harper and Row, 1981.

———. *Sweet Medicine: The Continuing Role of the Sacred Arrows, the Sun Dance, and the Buffalo Hat in Northern Cheyenne History*. 2 vols. Norman: University of Oklahoma Press, 1969.

Sandoz, Mari. *Crazy Horse*. Lincoln: University of Nebraska Press, 1961.

Seymour, Flora W. *The Story of the Red Man*. New York: Tudor Publishing Co., 1934.

Starkey, Marion L. *The Cherokee Nation*. New York: Alfred A. Knopf, 1946.

Underhill, Ruth. *Here Come the Navaho*. Washington, D.C.: U.S. Department of the Interior, Bureau of Indian Affairs, 1953.

Utley, Robert M. *The Last Days of the Sioux Nation*. New Haven, Conn.: Yale University Press, 1963.

Washburn, Wilcomb E., ed. *The Indian and the White Man*. New York: Doubleday and

Co., 1964.

Wellman, Paul I. *Glory, God, and Gold*. New York: Doubleday and Co., 1954.

Willison, George P. *Saints and Strangers*. New York: Reynal and Hitchcock, 1945.

OFFICIAL DOCUMENTS AND DOCUMENTARY REPORTS

Bureau of American Ethnology. Miscellaneous reports. Washington, D.C.: U.S. Government Printing Office.

Devereux, George. "Mohave Chiefdomship in Action: A Narrative of the Contacts of the Mohave Indians with the United States." *Plateau* 23, no. 3 (1951): 33– 43.

Hodge, Frederick Webb, ed. *Handbook of American Indians*. 2 vols. Washington, D.C.: Smithsonian Institution, 1906.

Rose, L. J., Jr. *L. J. Rose of Sunny Slope, 1827–1899*. San Marino, Calif.: Huntington Library, 1959.

U.S. Congress. House. *Wagon Road from Fort Defiance to the Colorado River*. Report of E. F. Beale to John B. Floyd, U.S. Secretary of War, April 26, 1858. *House Executive Document 124*, 35th Cong., 1st sess., 1858.

U.S. Congress. Senate. *Report of Explorations for a Railway Route, Near the 35th Parallel of North Latitude, from the Mississippi River to the Pacific Ocean*. Report of Lieutenant A. W. Whipple, assisted by Lieutenant Joseph C. Ives, U. S. Army Corps of Topographical Engineers. *Senate Executive Document 78*, 33rd Cong., 2nd sess., 1855.

U. S. Congress. Senate. *Report Upon the Colorado River of the West*. Report by Joseph C. Ives. *Senate Executive Document*, 36th Cong., 1st sess., 1861.

Woodward, Arthur. "Irataba — 'Chief of the Mohave.' " *Plateau* 25, no. 3 (1953): 53– 68.